PRENTICE HALL MATHEMATICS

GEOMETRY

Study Guide & Practice Workbook

PEARSON

Prentice
Hall

Boston, Massachusetts
Upper Saddle River, New Jersey

ISBN: 0-13-125453-7
12 13 14   09 08 07

Study Guide & Practice Workbook

Contents

Answers appear in the back of each Grab & Go File.

Contents (cont.)

Reteaching 1-1

OBJECTIVE: Using inductive reasoning to make conjectures	**MATERIALS:** Pennies

Example

Describe the next two figures in the sequence.

, , , . . .

Each pile of pennies has two more than the preceding pile, so the next pile
will have seven pennies, followed by a pile of nine pennies.

Exercises

**Use pennies to model the next two figures in each sequence. Then draw a
sketch of the two new figures. Show a maximum of ten coins in one stack.**

1. , . . .

2. , . . .

3.  , . . .

4. , . . .

5. , , , . . .

6. , , , . . .

Practice 1-1

Patterns and Inductive Reasoning

Find a pattern for each sequence. Use the pattern to show the next two terms.

1. 17, 23, 29, 35, 41, . . .

2. 1.01, 1.001, 1.0001, . . .

3. 12, 14, 18, 24, 32, . . .

4. 2, −4, 8, −16, 32, . . .

5. 1, 2, 4, 7, 11, 16, . . .

6. 32, 48, 56, 60, 62, 63, . . .

Name two different ways to continue each pattern.

7. 1, 1, 2, _?_

8. 48, 49, 50, _?_

9. 2, 4, _?_

10. A, B, C, . . . , Z, _?_

11. D, E, F, _?_

12. A, Z, B, _?_

Draw the next figure in each sequence.

13.   ____?____

14.   ____?____

15.

Seven people meet and shake hands with one another.

16. How many handshakes occur?

17. Using inductive reasoning, write a formula for the number of handshakes if the number of people is *n*.

The Fibonacci sequence consists of the pattern 1, 1, 2, 3, 5, 8, 13, . . .

18. What is the ninth term in the pattern?

19. Using your calculator, look at the successive ratios of one term to the next. Make a conjecture.

20. List the first eight terms of the sequence formed by finding the differences of successive terms in the Fibonacci sequence.

Reteaching 1-2

OBJECTIVE: Understanding basic terms and postulates of geometry	**MATERIALS:** Colored pencils or markers

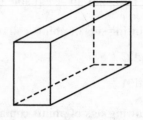

Example

Label the figure at the right as indicated.

a. Label three points that are coplanar as *A*, *B*, and *C*.

b. Label three points that are collinear as *X*, *Y*, and *Z*.

c. Trace two intersecting lines, and label their point of intersection as *T*.

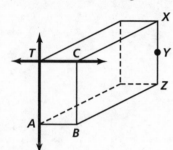

Exercises

Using colored pencils, label and shade the figure at the right as indicated.

1. With a yellow pencil, shade a plane. Then label three noncollinear points on the plane as *R, S,* and *T*.

2. With an orange pencil, shade a plane that intersects the plane you shaded yellow.

3. Describe the intersection of the planes you shaded yellow and orange.

4. With a red pencil, label four points that are coplanar as *E, F, G,* and *H*.

5. With a blue pencil, label three points that are collinear as *P, Q,* and *R*.

6. With a brown pencil, label four points that are not coplanar as *W, X, Y,* and *Z*.

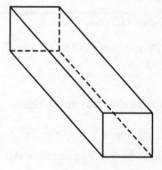

Use the grid at the right.

7. Graph the following points on the grid:
$P(-1, -1)$, $Q(0, 4)$, $R(-3, -5)$, $S(2, 5)$, and $T(3, -4)$.

8. Name three noncollinear points.

9. Name three collinear points.

10. Name two intersecting lines.

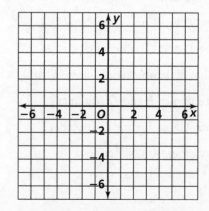

Practice 1-2

Points, Lines, and Planes

Refer to the diagram at the right for Exercises 1–15.

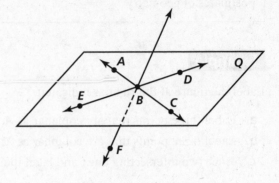

1. Name $\overleftrightarrow{AB}$ in another way.

2. Give two other names for plane Q.

3. Why is EBD not an acceptable name for plane Q?

Are the following sets of points collinear?

4. $\overleftrightarrow{AB}$ and C
5. B and F

6. $\overleftrightarrow{EB}$ and A
7. F and plane Q

Are the following sets of points coplanar?

8. E, B, and F
9. $\overleftrightarrow{DB}$ and $\overrightarrow{FC}$

10. $\overleftrightarrow{AC}$ and $\overleftrightarrow{ED}$
11. $\overleftrightarrow{AE}$ and $\overleftrightarrow{DC}$

12. F, A, B, and C
13. F, A, B, and D

14. plane Q and $\overleftrightarrow{EC}$
15. $\overrightarrow{FB}$ and $\overleftrightarrow{BD}$

Find the intersection of the following lines and planes in the figure at the right.

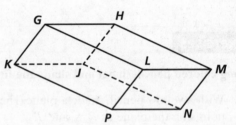

16. $\overleftrightarrow{GK}$ and $\overleftrightarrow{LG}$

17. planes GLM and LPN

18. planes $GHPN$ and KJP

19. planes HJN and GKL

20. $\overleftrightarrow{KP}$ and plane KJN

21. $\overleftrightarrow{KM}$ and plane GHL

Refer to the diagram at the right.

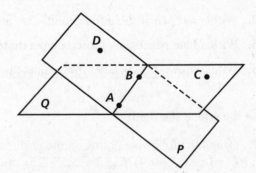

22. Name plane P in another way.

23. Name plane Q in another way.

24. What is the intersection of planes P and Q?

25. Are A and C collinear?

26. Are D, A, B, and C coplanar?

27. Are D and C collinear?

28. What is the intersection of $\overleftrightarrow{AB}$ and $\overleftrightarrow{DC}$?

29. Are planes P and Q coplanar?

30. Are $\overleftrightarrow{AB}$ and plane Q coplanar?

31. Are B and C collinear?

Reteaching 1-3

Segments, Rays, Parallel Lines, and Planes

OBJECTIVE: Recognizing parallel lines and parallel planes	**MATERIALS:** None

Example

Name two pairs of parallel lines.

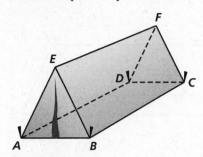

$\overleftrightarrow{EF}$ and $\overleftrightarrow{BC}$ are parallel because they are coplanar lines that do not intersect.
So are $\overleftrightarrow{AE}$ and $\overleftrightarrow{DF}$.

Exercises

For Exercises 1–7, name the lines or planes indicated.

1. Name a pair of parallel lines.

2. Name a pair of skew lines.

3. Name a pair of lines that are neither parallel lines nor skew lines.

4. Name a pair of parallel planes.

5. Name a pair of planes that intersect in a line.

6. Name three planes that intersect at a point.

7. Name a pair of skew lines different from the pair named in Exercise 2.

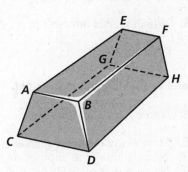

Draw a sketch for each of the following.

8. three parallel lines

9. two skew lines

10. two intersecting planes

11. two parallel planes

12. three intersecting lines

13. two parallel planes intersected by a line

Practice 1-3

Segments, Rays, Parallel Lines, and Planes

Write *true* or *false*.

1. $\overleftrightarrow{XY}$ is the same as $\overleftrightarrow{YX}$.

2. $\overrightarrow{XY}$ is the same as $\overrightarrow{YX}$.

3. If $\overrightarrow{AB}$ and $\overrightarrow{AC}$ are opposite rays, then they are collinear.

4. If two rays have the same endpoint, then they form a line.

5. If the union of two rays is a line, then the rays are opposite rays.

6. If $\overrightarrow{PQ}$ and $\overrightarrow{PR}$ are the same rays, then Q and R are the same point.

Refer to the diagram at the right.

7. Name all segments parallel to $\overline{EF}$.

8. Name all segments parallel to $\overline{FG}$.

9. Name three pairs of skew lines.

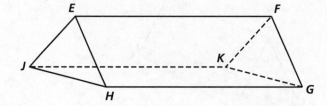

Refer to the diagram at the right.

10. Which pair(s) of planes is (are) parallel?

11. Which pair(s) of planes intersect?

12. Which planes intersect in $\overleftrightarrow{MN}$?

13. Which planes intersect in $\overleftrightarrow{RS}$?

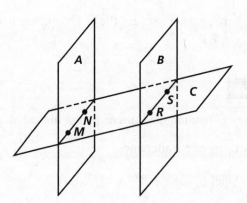

Refer to the diagram at the right.

14. Name $\overrightarrow{EF}$ in another way.

15. How many different segments can be named?

16. Name a pair of opposite rays with E as an endpoint.

17. Name in two different ways the ray opposite $\overrightarrow{FG}$.

18. Name $\overrightarrow{GE}$ in two other ways.

19. Are $\overline{EG}$ and $\overline{GE}$ the same segment?

Draw each of the following.

20. parallel planes S, T, and U

21. planes R and W intersecting in $\overleftrightarrow{PQ}$

Reteaching 1-4

OBJECTIVE: Finding the measure of an angle	**MATERIALS:** Protractor

Example

Measure and classify each angle formed by the five points of the star.

Measuring with a protractor shows that each angle is about 36°. Because each angle is less than 90°, each angle is an acute angle.

Exercises

The small stars illustrate which type of angle to measure. Use the large star when actually measuring the angles.

1. **a.** Measure the five angles on the inside of the pentagon that is formed.
   b. Classify each angle you measured.

2. **a.** Measure two of the angles on the outside of the pentagon that is formed.
   b. Classify each angle you measured.

3. **a.** Measure the five angles between two points of the star.
   b. Classify each angle you measured.

Measure and classify each angle.

4.   5. 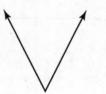   6.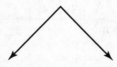

7. 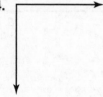   8. 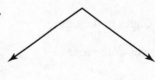   9.

Practice 1-4

If *GJ* = 32, find the value of each of the following.

1. *x*

2. *GH*

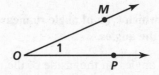

3. *HJ*

4. Find *PD* if the coordinate of *P* is −7 and the coordinate of *D* is −1.

5. Find *SK* if the coordinate of *S* is 17 and the coordinate of *K* is −5.

6. Find the coordinate of *B* if *AB* = 8 and the coordinate of *A* is −2.

7. Find the coordinate of *X* if *XY* = 1 and the coordinate of *Y* is 0.

8. Name the angle at the right in three different ways.

If *AX* = 45, find the value of each of the following.

9. *y*

10. *AQ*

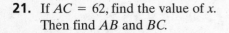

11. *QX*

Find the measure of each angle.

12. ∠*EBF*   13. ∠*EBA*

14. ∠*DBE*   15. ∠*DBC*

16. ∠*ABF*   17. ∠*DBF*

18. Name all acute angles in the figure.

19. Name all obtuse angles in the figure.

20. Name all right angles in the figure.

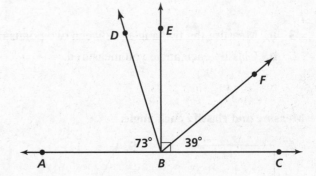

21. If *AC* = 62, find the value of *x*.
    Then find *AB* and *BC*.

22. If *AC* = 206, find the value of *x*.
    Then find *AB* and *BC*.

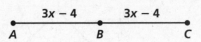

Reteaching 1-5

Basic Constructions

OBJECTIVE: Using a compass and straightedge to construct angles	**MATERIALS:** Compass, straightedge

Example

Construct $\angle TRQ$ so that $m\angle TRQ = m\angle X + m\angle Y$.

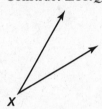 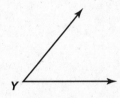

First, construct $\angle PRQ$ so that $m\angle PRQ = m\angle X$.

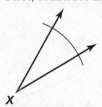 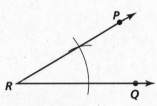

Second, construct $\angle TRP$ so that $m\angle TRP = m\angle Y$.

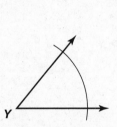 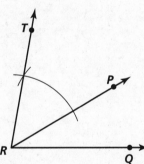

Then, $m\angle TRQ = m\angle PRQ + m\angle TRP$, so $m\angle TRQ = m\angle X + m\angle Y$.

Exercises

Use the diagrams at the right for the following constructions.

1. $\angle CAB$ so that $m\angle CAB = m\angle 1 + m\angle 2$

2. $\angle QRS$ so that $m\angle QRS = m\angle 2 - m\angle 1$

3. $\angle XYZ$ so that $m\angle XYZ = 2m\angle 1$

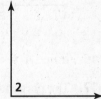

Use the diagrams at the right for the following constructions.

4. $\angle DEF$ so that $m\angle DEF = m\angle 3 + m\angle 4$

5. $\angle TUV$ so that $m\angle TUV = m\angle 3 - m\angle 4$

6. $\angle JKL$ so that $m\angle JKL = \frac{1}{2}m\angle 3$

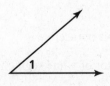

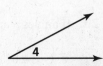

Practice 1-5

Construct each figure as directed.

1. Construct $\overline{AB}$ congruent to $\overline{XY}$. Check your work with a ruler.

2. Construct the perpendicular bisector of $\overline{XY}$.

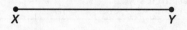

3. Construct a triangle whose sides are all the same length as $\overline{XY}$.

4. Construct the angle bisector of $\angle Z$.

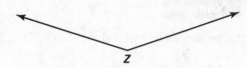

Check your work with a protractor.

5. **a.** Construct a 90° angle.

   b. Construct a 45° angle.

6. Construct $\overline{AB}$ so that $AB = MN + OP$.

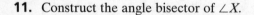

7. Construct $\overline{KL}$ so that $KL = OP - MN$.

8. Construct $\angle A$ so that $m\angle A = m\angle 1 + m\angle 2$.

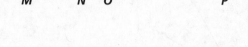

9. Construct $\angle B$ so that $m\angle B = m\angle 1 - m\angle 2$.

10. Construct $\angle C$ so that $m\angle C = 2m\angle 2$.

11. Construct the angle bisector of $\angle X$.

12. Construct $\angle W$ so that $m\angle W = 2m\angle X$.

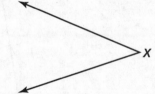

13. Construct $\angle Z$ so that $m\angle Z = \frac{1}{2}m\angle X$.

Write *true* or *false*.

14. $\overline{AB} \cong \overline{XY}$

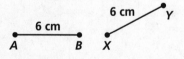

15. $m\angle 1 = 40$

16. If $m\angle A = 80$, then $\angle A$ is obtuse.

17. The perpendicular bisector of a line segment creates four 90° angles.

18. If $m\angle 1 = 45$ and $m\angle 2 = m\angle 1$, then $m\angle 1 + m\angle 2 = 90$.

19. For a given $\angle A$, $\frac{1}{2} \cdot m\angle A = 2 \cdot m\angle A$.

20. If angles 3 and 4 are complementary and $m\angle 3 = m\angle 4$, then $m\angle 4 = 45$.

Reteaching 1-6

The Coordinate Plane

OBJECTIVE: Finding the distance between two points in the coordinate plane

MATERIALS: Graph paper, ruler

Example

Show that the sum of the lengths of the two shortest sides of the triangle is greater than the length of the third side.

Use the distance formula: $d = \sqrt{(x_2 - x_1)^2 + (y_2 - y_1)^2}$

$BA = \sqrt{(2 - (-1))^2 + (4 - 2)^2}$ $AC = \sqrt{(-1 - 4)^2 + (2 - (-1))^2}$

     $= \sqrt{3^2 + 2^2}$ $= \sqrt{(-5)^2 + 3^2}$

     $= \sqrt{9 + 4}$ $= \sqrt{25 + 9}$

     $= \sqrt{13}$ $= \sqrt{34}$

     ≈ 3.6 ≈ 5.8

$BC = \sqrt{(2 - 4)^2 + (4 - (-1))^2}$

     $= \sqrt{(-2)^2 + 5^2}$

     $= \sqrt{4 + 25}$

     $= \sqrt{29}$

     ≈ 5.4

$3.6 + 5.4 > 5.8$, so $BA + BC > AC$.

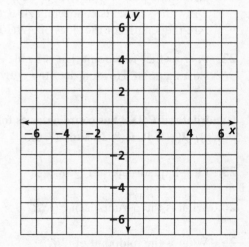

Exercises

Use the grid at the right.

1. Graph the coordinates $X(-2, 4)$, $Y(6, -3)$, and $Z(2, -2)$. Connect the vertices to form a triangle.

2. Find the lengths of the sides $\overline{XY}$, $\overline{YZ}$, and $\overline{XZ}$ to the nearest tenth.

3. Show that the sum of the lengths of the two shortest sides is greater than the length of the third side.

Find the distance between the points to the nearest tenth.

4. $A(-2, -5)$, $B(-4, 7)$

5. $R(3, -4)$, $S(-1, 3)$

6. $G(-4, -5)$, $H(3, 2)$

7. $C(2, 5)$, $D(5, -6)$

8. $E(-7, 3)$, $F(0, 9)$

9. $J(-11, -4)$, $K(-3, -1)$

10. $X(0, 10)$, $Y(-6, -7)$

11. $L(5, -6)$, $M(8, 2)$

12. $U(9, 3)$, $V(9, -14)$

Practice 1-6

The Coordinate Plane

Graph each point in the coordinate plane.

1. $A(-2, 5)$ **2.** $B(5, -2)$ **3.** $C(0, 6)$ **4.** $D(-4, 0)$ **5.** $E(-4, -2)$

Find the distance between the points to the nearest tenth.

6. $L(-4, 11), M(-3, 4)$ **7.** $N(1, 0), P(3, 8)$

8. $Q(10, 10), R(10, -2)$ **9.** $S(0, 5), T(0, -3)$

10. $U(11, 0), V(-1, 0)$ **11.** $W(2, 7), X(1, 2)$

Find the coordinates of the midpoint of each segment. The coordinates of the endpoints are given.

12. $A(6, 7), B(4, 3)$ **13.** $C(-1, 5), D(2, -3)$

14. $E(14, -2), F(7, -8)$ **15.** $O(0, 0), G(-5, 12)$

16. $H(2.8, 1.1), I(-3.4, 5.7)$ **17.** $J(2\frac{1}{2}, -\frac{1}{4}), K(3\frac{1}{4}, -1)$

18. The midpoint of $\overline{AB}$ is $(1, 2)$. The coordinates of A are $(-3, 6)$. Find the coordinates of B.

19. The midpoint of $\overline{CD}$ is $(4, 11)$. The coordinates of D are $(4, 12)$. Find the coordinates of C.

20. The midpoint of $\overline{EF}$ is $(-3, 7)$. The coordinates of E are $(-3, 10)$. Find the coordinates of F.

21. Graph the points $A(2, 1), B(2, -5), C(-4, -5),$ and $D(-4, 1)$. Draw the segments connecting $A, B, C,$ and D in order. Are the lengths of the sides of $ABCD$ the same? Explain.

22. A crow flies to a point that is 1 mile east and 20 miles south of its starting point. How far does the crow fly?

Quadrilateral *PQSR* has coordinates as follows: *P*(0, 0), *Q*(−1, 4), *R*(8, 2), and *S*(7, 6).

23. Graph quadrilateral *PQSR*.

24. What is the perimeter of *PQSR*?

25. What is the midpoint of $\overline{QR}$?

Name _____ Class _____ Date _____

Reteaching 1-7

Perimeter, Circumference, and Area

OBJECTIVE: Finding area and perimeter of squares, rectangles, and circles	**MATERIALS:** Graph paper

Example

A rectangle has an area of 48 square units. Its base and height are integers. Use graph paper to determine possible dimensions of the rectangle.

Because the base and height are integers, they must be factors of 48.

List all the factors of 48: 1, 2, 3, 4, 6, 8, 12, 16, 24, and 48. Use the factors to draw possible rectangles on graph paper.

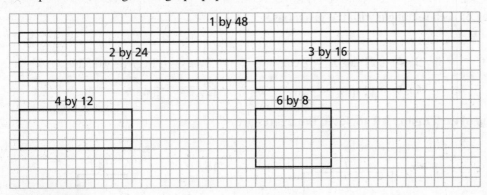

Exercises

Solve for the indicated perimeter or area.

1. **a.** A rectangle has an area of 60 square units. If its base and height are integers, what are its possible dimensions? Sketch each rectangle on graph paper.

   b. Find the perimeter of each rectangle.

2. **a.** A rectangle has an area of 36 square units. If its base and height are integers, what are its possible dimensions? Sketch each rectangle on graph paper.

   b. Which of the possible rectangles has the greatest perimeter?

3. Find the dimensions of a rectangle having the least possible perimeter when its base and height are integers and its area is 18 cm^2.

Draw a circle on graph paper so that the center is at the intersection of grid lines.

4. What is the diameter of your circle? What is the radius of your circle?

5. Estimate the area of the circle by counting the number of squares and parts of squares in the circle.

6. Calculate the area of your circle, using the formula. Round your answer to the nearest tenth.

7. How does your calculated result compare with your estimated result?

Practice 1-7

Find the area of each rectangle with the given base and height.

1. base: 3 ft
height: 22 in.

2. base: 60 in.
height: 1.5 yd

3. base: 2 m
height: 120 cm

Find the circumference of each circle in terms of π.

4.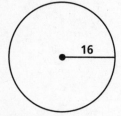

5.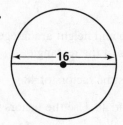

6.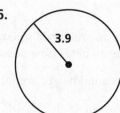

Find the perimeter and area of each rectangle with the given base and height.

7. $b = 7$ cm, $h = 6$ cm

8. $b = 21$ cm, $h = 2$ cm

9. $b = 4$ in., $h = 10.5$ in.

10. $b = 17$ ft, $h = 3$ ft

11. $b = 11$ m, $h = 9$ m

12. $b = 13$ m, $h = 7$ m

Find the perimeter and area of each figure. All angles in the figures are right angles.

13.

14.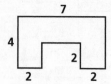

15.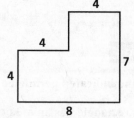

Find the area of each circle in terms of π.

16.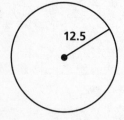

17.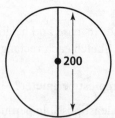

18.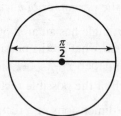

19. Find the area and perimeter of rectangle $ABCD$ with vertices $A(3, 7)$, $B(9, 7)$, $C(9, -1)$, and $D(3, -1)$.

20. Find the perimeter of $\triangle PQR$ with vertices $P(-2, 9)$, $Q(7, -3)$, and $R(-2, -3)$.

21. The circumference of a circle is 26π. Find the diameter and the radius.

Reteaching 2-1

OBJECTIVE: Writing the converse of conditional statements	**MATERIALS:** None

Example

Write the converse of the following statement.

If snow is falling, then the temperature is below freezing.

If snow is falling, then the temperature is below freezing.

      hypothesis   conclusion

Converse: Interchange hypothesis and conclusion.
             If the temperature is below freezing, then snow is falling.

Exercises

**Work in groups of three. Each group member should make up three
conditionals relating to sports, hobbies, school, or mathematics.**

1. Working alone, write the converse for each conditional.

2. Determine whether each converse is true.

3. Compare your answers with those of the other members of your group.
Revise your work until you all agree.

**Write the converse for each of the following conditionals. Determine the
truth value of each conditional and its converse.**

4. If you see lightning, then you hear thunder.

5. If your pants are blue, then they are jeans.

6. If you are eating an orange fruit, then you are eating a tangerine.

7. If a number is a whole number, then it is an integer.

8. If a triangle is an obtuse triangle, then it has one angle greater than 90°.

9. If $n = 8$, then $n^2 = 64$.

10. If you got an A on the first test, then you got an A for the quarter.

11. If a figure is a square, then it has four sides.

12. If $\sqrt{x} = 12$, then $x = 144$.

Practice 2-1

Show that each conditional is false by finding a counterexample.

1. If it is 12:00 noon, then the sun is shining.

2. If the car is full of gas, then the engine will start.

3. If a number is divisible by 3, then it is odd.

Write the converse of each conditional.

4. If you drink milk, then you will be strong.

5. If a rectangle has four sides the same length, then it is a square.

6. If you do not sleep, you will be tired.

Write the converse of each statement. If the converse is true, write *true*; if it is not true, provide a counterexample.

7. If $x - 4 = 22$, then $x = 26$.

8. If $|x| > 0$, then $x > 0$.

9. If m^2 is positive, then m is positive.

10. If $y = 3$, then $2y - 1 = 5$.

11. If point A is in the first quadrant of a coordinate grid, then $x > 0$.

12. If two lines have equal slopes, then the lines are parallel.

13. If you are a twin, then you have a sibling.

14. Draw a Venn diagram to illustrate the statement in Exercise 13.

Answer the following questions about the given quote.

"If you like to shop, then visit the Pigeon Forge outlets in Tennessee."

15. Identify the hypothesis and the conclusion.

16. What does the quote suggest about the Pigeon Forge outlets?

17. Write the converse of the conditional.

18. Is the converse of the conditional a true statement? Explain your reasoning.

Answer the following questions about the billboard advertisement shown.

19. What does the billboard imply?

20. Write the advertisement slogan as a conditional statement.

21. Write the converse of the conditional statement from Exercise 20.

Train **harder**, run **faster** with **SUSTAIN**

Reteaching 2-2

OBJECTIVE: Writing biconditional statements and identifying good definitions	**MATERIALS:** None

Example 1

Consider the true statement given below. Write its converse. If the converse is also true, combine the statements as a biconditional.

Conditional: If a pentagon has five equal sides, then it is an equilateral pentagon.

Converse: If a pentagon is an equilateral pentagon, then it has five equal sides.

The converse is true, so the two statements can be written as one biconditional.

Biconditional: A pentagon is an equilateral pentagon if and only if it has five equal sides.

Example 2

Show that this definition of isosceles triangle is a good definition. Then write it as a true biconditional. *An isosceles triangle has two sides of equal length.*

Conditional: If a triangle has two sides of equal length, then it is an isosceles triangle.

Converse: If a triangle is isosceles, then it has two sides of equal length.

Because the two conditionals are true, this is a good definition and can be rewritten as a biconditional.

Biconditional: A triangle is an isosceles triangle if and only if two sides are of equal length.

Exercises

Write the two conditional statements that make up each biconditional.

1. $|n| = 15$ if and only if $n = 15$ or $n = -15$.

2. Two segments are congruent if and only if they have the same measure.

3. You live in California if and only if you live in the most populated state in the United States.

4. An integer is a multiple of 10 if and only if the last digit is 0.

If the statement is a good definition, write it as a biconditional. If not, find a counterexample.

5. An elephant is a large animal.

6. Two planes intersect at a line.

7. An even number is a number that ends in 0, 2, 4, 6, or 8.

8. A triangle is a three-sided figure whose angle measures sum to 180°.

Practice 2-2

Each conditional statement is true. Consider each converse. If the converse is true, combine the statements and write them as a biconditional.

1. If two angles have the same measure, then they are congruent.

2. If $2x - 5 = 11$, then $x = 8$.

3. If $n = 17$, then $|n| = 17$.

4. If a figure has eight sides, then it is an octagon.

Write the two conditional statements that make up each biconditional.

5. A whole number is a multiple of 5 if and only if its last digit is either a 0 or a 5.

6. Two lines are perpendicular if and only if they intersect to form four right angles.

7. You live in Texas if and only if you live in the largest state in the contiguous United States.

Explain why each of the following is not an acceptable definition.

8. An automobile is a motorized vehicle with four wheels.

9. A circle is a shape that is round.

10. The median of a set of numbers is larger than the smallest number in the set and smaller than the largest number in the set.

11. Cricket is a game played on a large field with a ball and a bat.

12. A rectangle is a very pleasing shape with smooth sides and very rigid corners.

Some figures that are *piggles* are shown below, as are some *nonpiggles*.

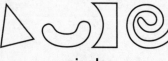

piggles

nonpiggles

Tell whether each of the following is a *piggle*.

13. [figure]

14. [figure]

15.

Reteaching 2-3

OBJECTIVE: Using the Law of Detachment and the Law of Syllogism to draw conclusions	MATERIALS: None

Example 1

Use the Law of Detachment to draw a conclusion.

> If a person goes to the zoo, he or she will see animals.   *conditional*
> Karla goes to the zoo.   *hypothesis of conditional*

Both the conditional and hypothesis are given to be true. By the Law of Detachment, the conclusion is that Karla will see animals.

However, the Law of Detachment does not apply when a conditional and a *conclusion* are given. Consider the following:

> If a person goes to the zoo, he or she will see animals.   *conditional*
> Karla sees animals.   *conclusion of conditional*

The Law of Detachment cannot be used to say that Karla went to the zoo. In fact, Karla may have seen dogs in the park and not gone to the zoo at all. In this case, no conclusion is possible.

Example 2

Use the Law of Syllogism to draw a conclusion.

> If a polygon is a hexagon, then the sum of its angles is 720.   *conditional 1*
> If the sum of the angles of a polygon is 720, then it has six sides.   *conditional 2*

Both conditionals are given to be true. By the Law of Syllogism, if a polygon is a hexagon, then it has six sides.

Exercises

For each problem, tell which law may be used to draw a conclusion. Then write the conclusion. If a conclusion is not possible, write *not possible* and explain why.

1. If a person is driving over the speed limit, the police officer will give the person a ticket.
   Darlene is driving over the speed limit.

2. If two planes do not intersect, then they are parallel.
   If two planes do not have any points in common, then they do not intersect.

3. If the result of the arm X-ray is positive, then a bone is broken.
   The result of Landon's arm X-ray is positive.

4. If you live in Chicago, then you live in Illinois.
   Brad lives in Illinois.

5. If a figure is a circle, then its circumference is πd.
   Tony draws a circle with a diameter (*d*) of 1 inch.

Practice 2-3

Use the Law of Detachment to draw a conclusion.

1. If the measures of two angles have a sum of 90°, then the angles are complementary.

    $m\angle A + m\angle B = 90$

2. If the football team wins on Friday night, then practice is canceled for Monday.

    The football team won by 7 points on Friday night.

3. If a triangle has one 90° angle, then the triangle is a right triangle.

    In $\triangle DEF$, $m\angle E = 90$.

Use the Law of Syllogism to draw a conclusion.

4. If you liked the movie, then you saw a good movie.

    If you saw a good movie, then you enjoyed yourself.

5. If two lines are not parallel, then they intersect.

    If two lines intersect, then they intersect at a point.

6. If you vacation at the beach, then you must like the ocean.

    If you like the ocean, then you will like Florida.

If possible, use the Law of Detachment to draw a conclusion. If not possible, write _not possible_.

7. If Robbie wants to save money to buy a car, he must get a part-time job.

    Robbie started a new job yesterday at a grocery store.

8. If a person lives in Omaha, then he or she lives in Nebraska.

    Tamika lives in Omaha.

9. If two figures are congruent, their areas are equal.

    The area of $ABCD$ equals the area of $PQRS$.

Use the Law of Detachment and the Law of Syllogism to draw conclusions from the following statements.

10. If it is raining, the temperature is greater than 32°F.

    If the temperature is greater than 32°F, then it is not freezing outside.

    It is raining.

11. If you live in Providence, then you live in Rhode Island.

    If you live in Rhode Island, then you live in the smallest state in the United States.

    Shannon lives in Providence.

12. If it does not rain, the track team will have practice.

    If the track team has practice, the team members will warm up by jogging two miles.

    It does not rain on Thursday.

Reteaching 2-4

Reasoning in Algebra

OBJECTIVE: Naming and ordering properties used in algebraic reasoning

MATERIALS: None

Example

Use the figure to solve for x. Justify each step.

Given: $JL = 62$

$JK + KL = JL$	Segment Addition Postulate
$5x + (8x - 3) = 62$	Substitution Property
$13x - 3 = 62$	Simplify
$13x = 65$	Addition Property of Equality
$x = 5$	Division Property of Equality

Exercises

Name the properties that justify the steps taken.

1. $AB = EF$; therefore $AB + CD = EF + CD$.

2. $\angle ABC \cong \angle Q$; therefore $\angle Q \cong \angle ABC$.

Support each statement with a reason.

3. $5(y - x) = 20$ Given

    $5y - 5x = 20$?

4. $2x = m\angle C + x$ Given

    $x = m\angle C$?

5. $CD = AF - 2(CD)$ Given

    $3(CD) = AF$?

6. $(q - x) = r$ Given

    $4(q - x) = 4r$?

7. $m\angle Q - m\angle R = 90$ Given

    $m\angle Q = 4m\angle R$ Given

    $4m\angle R - m\angle R = 90$?

8. $m\angle AOX = 2m\angle XOB$ Given

    $2m\angle XOB = 140$ Given

    $m\angle AOX = 140$?

9. $m\angle P + m\angle Q = 90$ and $m\angle Q = 5m\angle P$. Order the steps given below to show that $m\angle Q = 75$.

   1. By the Distributive Property, $6m\angle P = 90$.

   2. By substitution, $m\angle Q = 5 \times 15 = 75$.

   3. By the Division Property, $m\angle P = 15$.

   4. Given: $m\angle P + m\angle Q = 90$, $m\angle Q = 5m\angle P$.

   5. By substitution, $m\angle P + 5m\angle P = 90$.

Practice 2-4

Use the given property to complete each statement.

1. Symmetric Property of Equality
   If $MN = UT$, then __?__.

2. Division Property of Equality
   If $4m\angle QWR = 120$, then __?__.

3. Transitive Property of Equality
   If $SB = VT$ and $VT = MN$, then __?__.

4. Addition Property of Equality
   If $y - 15 = 36$, then __?__.

5. Reflexive Property of Congruence
   $\overline{JL} \cong$ __?__

Give a reason for each step.

6. $7x - 4 = 10$
    $7x = 14$
    $x = 2$

7. $0.25x + 2x + 12 = 39$
    $2.25x + 12 = 39$
    $2.25x = 27$
    $225x = 2700$
    $x = 12$

Name the property that justifies each statement.

8. If $m\angle G = 35$ and $m\angle S = 35$, then $m\angle G \cong m\angle S$.

9. If $10x + 6y = 14$ and $x = 2y$, then $10(2y) + 6y = 14$.

10. If $TR = MN$ and $MN = VW$, then $TR = VW$.

11. If $\overline{JK} \cong \overline{LM}$, then $\overline{LM} \cong \overline{JK}$.

12. If $\angle Q \cong \angle S$ and $\angle S \cong \angle P$, then $\angle Q \cong \angle P$.

Fill in the missing information. Solve for x, and justify each step.

13.

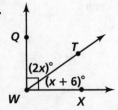

$m\angle QWT + m\angle TWX = 90$
$2x + (x + 6) =$ __?__
__?__ $+ 6 = 90$
__?__ $=$ __?__
$x =$ __?__

14.

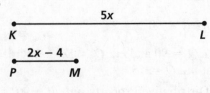

$KL = 3(PM)$
$5x = 3$ __?__
$5x =$ __?__
__?__ $= -12$
$x =$ __?__

Reteaching 2-5

Proving Angles Congruent

OBJECTIVE: Using deductive reasoning to solve problems and verify conjectures

MATERIALS: None

Example

Suppose that two complementary angles are congruent. Prove that the measure of each angle is 45.

Given: $\angle 1$ and $\angle 2$ are complementary.

$m\angle 1 = m\angle 2$

Prove: $m\angle 1 = 45$ and $m\angle 2 = 45$

By the definition of complementary angles, $m\angle 1 + m\angle 2 = 90$. By substitution, $m\angle 1 + m\angle 1 = 90$. Using the Addition Property of Equality, $2m\angle 1 = 90$. Using the Division Property of Equality, $m\angle 1 = 45$. By substitution, $m\angle 2 = 45$.

Exercises

In the diagram, $m\angle 1 = m\angle 3$. Order the steps given below to prove that $m\angle 2 = m\angle 4$.

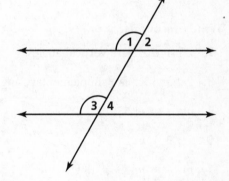

1. By the Angle Addition Postulate, $m\angle 3 + m\angle 4 = 180$.

2. Prove: $m\angle 2 = m\angle 4$

3. By substitution, $m\angle 3 + m\angle 2 = m\angle 3 + m\angle 4$.

4. By the Angle Addition Postulate, $m\angle 1 + m\angle 2 = 180$.

5. Given: $m\angle 1 = m\angle 3$

6. $m\angle 1 + m\angle 2 = m\angle 3 + m\angle 4$ by the Transitive Property of Equality.

7. Subtract $m\angle 3$ from both sides, and you get $m\angle 2 = m\angle 4$.

In the diagram, $\angle 7$ and $\angle 8$ are congruent, and $\angle 10$ is a right angle. Explain why each statement is true.

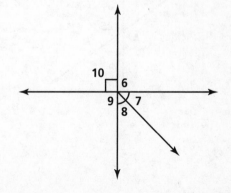

8. $m\angle 8 = 45$

9. $\angle 9$ and $\angle 10$ are supplementary.

10. $\angle 6$ is a right angle.

Practice 2-5

Proving Angles Congruent

Find the values of the variables.

1.
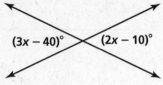
$(3x - 40)°$ $(2x - 10)°$

2.
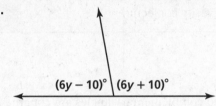
$(6y - 10)°$ $(6y + 10)°$

3.
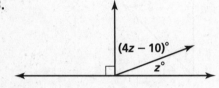
$(4z - 10)°$ $z°$

4.
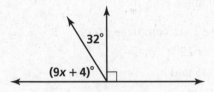
$32°$
$(9x + 4)°$

5.
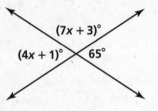
$(7x + 3)°$
$(4x + 1)°$ $65°$

6.
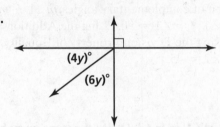
$(4y)°$
$(6y)°$

Write *true* or *false*.

7. $\angle 1$ and $\angle 2$ are vertical angles.

8. $\angle 2$ and $\angle 3$ are supplementary angles.

9. $m\angle 1 = m\angle 3$

10. $m\angle 3 + m\angle 4 = 180$

11. $m\angle 1 + m\angle 3 = 180$

12. $\angle 4$ and $\angle 2$ are adjacent angles.

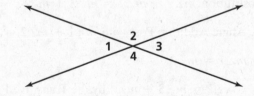

Write three conclusions that can be drawn from each figure.

13.
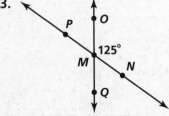

14.
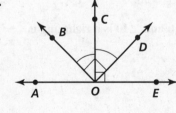

15.
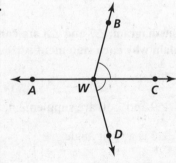

Reteaching 3-1

OBJECTIVE: Relating the measures of angles formed by parallel lines and a transversal

MATERIALS: Ruler, protractor

Example

If $m\angle 1 = 100$, find the measure of each of the other seven angles.

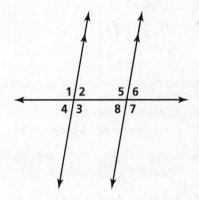

$m\angle 1 + m\angle 2 = 180; m\angle 2 = 80$	Supplementary angles
$m\angle 1 + m\angle 4 = 180; m\angle 4 = 80$	Supplementary angles
$\angle 1 \cong \angle 3; m\angle 3 = 100$	Vertical angles
$\angle 3 \cong \angle 5; m\angle 5 = 100$	Alternate interior angles
$m\angle 3 + m\angle 8 = 180; m\angle 8 = 80$	Same-side interior angles
$\angle 3 \cong \angle 7; m\angle 7 = 100$	Corresponding angles
$m\angle 6 + m\angle 7 = 180; m\angle 6 = 80$	Supplementary angles

Exercises

Complete the following to find measures of angles associated with a pair of parallel lines and a transversal.

1. **a.** Draw a pair of parallel lines using lined paper or the edges of a ruler. Then draw a transversal that intersects the two parallel lines.

    b. Use a protractor to measure one of the angles formed. Record the measure on your drawing.

    c. Find the measures of the other seven angles without measuring.

    d. Verify the angle measures by measuring each with a protractor.

Find the measure of each angle in the diagram at the right.

2. $m\angle 1$ 3. $m\angle 2$

4. $m\angle 4$ 5. $m\angle 5$

6. $m\angle 6$ 7. $m\angle 7$

8. $m\angle 8$

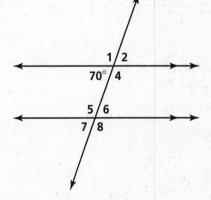

Practice 3-1

Classify each pair of angles as *alternate interior angles, same-side interior angles,* **or** *corresponding angles.*

1.

2.

3.

4.

5.

6.

Use the figure on the right to answer Exercises 7–9.

7. Name all pairs of corresponding angles formed by the transversal *t* and lines *s* and *c*.

8. Name all pairs of alternate interior angles formed by the transversal *t* and lines *s* and *c*.

9. Name all pairs of same-side interior angles formed by the transversal *t* and lines *s* and *c*.

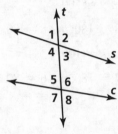

Find *m∠1* **and then** *m∠2.* **Justify each answer.**

10.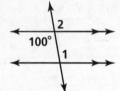

11.

12.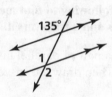

Algebra **Find the value of** *x.* **Then find the measure of each angle.**

13.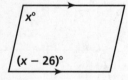

14.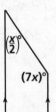

15.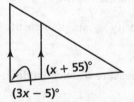

16. Developing Proof Supply the missing reasons in this two-column proof.

Given: *a* ∥ *b*

Prove: ∠1 ≅ ∠3

Statements	Reasons
1. *a* ∥ *b*	**1.** Given
2. ∠1 ≅ ∠2	**a.** ?
3. ∠2 ≅ ∠3	**b.** ?
4. ∠1 ≅ ∠3	**c.** ?

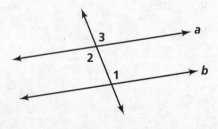

Reteaching 3-2

OBJECTIVE: Writing flow proofs   **MATERIALS:** None

Example

Write a flow proof for Theorem 3-1: If two parallel lines are cut by a
transversal, then alternate interior angles are congruent.

Given: $l \parallel m$

Prove: $\angle 2 \cong \angle 3$

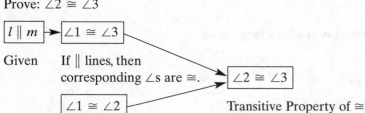

Vertical angles are $\cong$.

Exercises

1. Complete the flow proof for Theorem 3-2 using the following steps.
   Then write the reasons for each step.

   a. $\angle 2$ and $\angle 3$ are supplementary.   **b.** $\angle 1 \cong \angle 3$ **c.** $l \parallel m$

   d. $m\angle 1 + m\angle 2 = 180$ **e.** $m\angle 3 + m\angle 2 = 180$

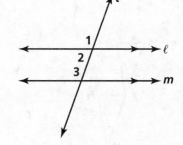

   Theorem 3-2: If two parallel lines are cut by a transversal, then same-
   side interior angles are supplementary.

   Given: $l \parallel m$

   Prove: $\angle 2$ and $\angle 3$ are supplementary.

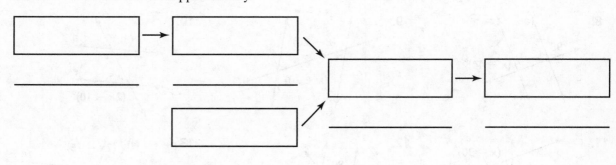

2. Write a flow proof for the following:

   Given: $\angle 2 \cong \angle 3$

   Prove: $a \parallel b$

Practice 3-2

1. **Developing Proof** Complete the paragraph proof for the figure shown.

Given: ∠RQT and ∠QTS are supplementary.
      ∠TSV and ∠SVU are supplementary.

Prove: $\overleftrightarrow{QR} \parallel \overleftrightarrow{UV}$

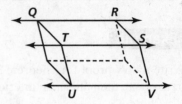

Proof Because ∠RQT and ∠QTS are supplementary, ∠RQT and ∠QTS are **a.** ? angles. By the Same-Side Interior Angles Theorem, **b.** ? ‖ **c.** ? . Because ∠TSV and ∠SVU are supplementary, ∠TSV and ∠SVU are **d.** ? angles. By the **e.** ? Theorem, $\overleftrightarrow{TS} \parallel \overleftrightarrow{UV}$. Because $\overleftrightarrow{QR}$ and $\overleftrightarrow{UV}$ both are parallel to **f.** ? , $\overleftrightarrow{QR} \parallel \overleftrightarrow{UV}$ by Theorem **g.** ? .

Which lines or segments are parallel? Justify your answer with a theorem or postulate.

2.
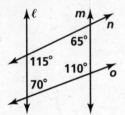

3.
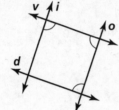

4.
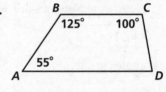

5.
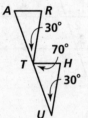

6.
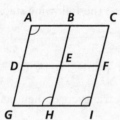

7.
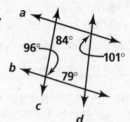

Algebra Find the value of *x* for which *a* ‖ *t*.

8.
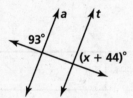

9.
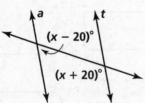

10.
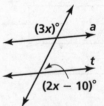

11.
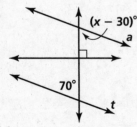

12.
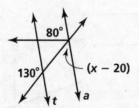

13.
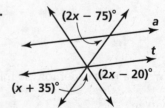

Reteaching 3-3

Parallel Lines and the Triangle Angle-Sum Theorem

• •

| **OBJECTIVE:** Classifying triangles and finding the measures of their angles | **MATERIALS:** Ruler |

Example

In the diagram at the right, *ACED* has four right angles. Find the missing angle measures in △*ABC*, and classify them. Then classify △*ABC* in as many ways as you can.

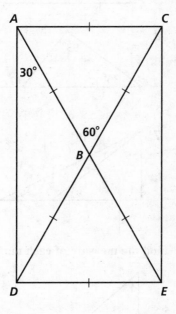

$$m\angle CAB + m\angle DAB = 90 \qquad \text{Angle Addition Postulate}$$
$$m\angle CAB + 30 = 90 \qquad \text{Substitution}$$
$$m\angle CAB = 60 \qquad \text{Subtraction Property of Equality}$$
$$m\angle ACB + m\angle CAB + m\angle ABC = 180 \qquad \text{Triangle Angle-Sum Theorem}$$
$$m\angle ACB + 60 + 60 = 180 \qquad \text{Substitution}$$
$$m\angle ACB + 120 = 80 \qquad \text{Addition}$$
$$m\angle ACB = 60 \qquad \text{Subtraction Property of Equality}$$

Because $m\angle CAB < 90$ and $m\angle ACB < 90$, $\angle CAB$ and $\angle ACB$ are acute.

Therefore, △*ABC* is equilateral, equiangular, and acute.

Exercises

Refer to the diagram above.

1. Find the missing angle measures in △*ABD*, △*CBE*, and △*BDE*.

2. Name the eight triangles in the diagram. Then sketch the triangles, and classify them in as many ways as possible. (△*ABC* has been classified in the example.)

In the diagram at the right, ∠RPT, ∠PTS, ∠TSR, and ∠SRP are right angles.

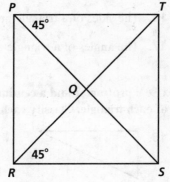

3. Find the missing angle measures in △*PQT*, △*PQR*, △*RQS*, and △*SQT*.

4. Measure the side lengths of △*PQT*, △*PQR*, △*RQS*, and △*SQT* to the nearest millimeter.

5. List and classify each triangle. (*Hint:* There are eight triangles.)

Practice 3-3

Parallel Lines and the Triangle Angle-Sum Theorem

Find the value of each variable.

1.
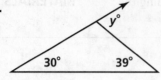

2.
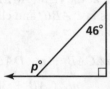

3.

4.
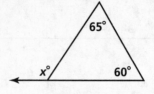

5.
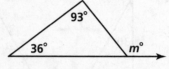

6.
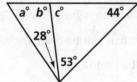

7.
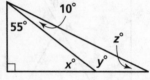

8.
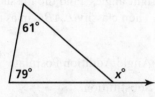

9.
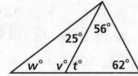

Find the measure of each numbered angle.

10.
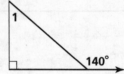

11.
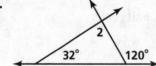

12.
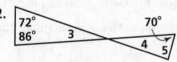

13.
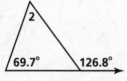

14.
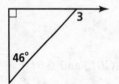

15.
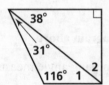

16. The sides of a triangle are 10 cm, 8 cm, and 10 cm. Classify the triangle.

17. The angles of a triangle are 44°, 110°, and 26°. Classify the triangle.

Use a protractor and a centimeter ruler to measure the angles and the sides of each triangle. Classify each triangle by its angles and sides.

18.

19.
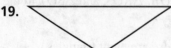

20.

Reteaching 3-4

OBJECTIVE: Finding the sum of the measures of the interior and exterior angles of polygons

MATERIALS: None

Example

A pattern of regular hexagons and regular pentagons covers a soccer ball. Find the measures of an interior and an exterior angle of the hexagon and an interior and an exterior angle of the pentagon.

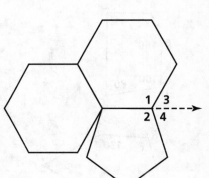

- The sum of the measures of the interior angles of a hexagon equals $(n - 2)180 = (6 - 2)180 = 720$.

- $m\angle 1 = 720 \div 6 = 120$.

- The sum of the measures of the exterior angles of a hexagon equals 360.

- $m\angle 3 = 360 \div 6 = 60$.

- The sum of the measures of the interior angles of a pentagon equals $(5 - 2)180 = 540$.

- $m\angle 2 = 540 \div 5 = 108$.

- The sum of the measures of the exterior angles of a pentagon equals 360.

- $m\angle 4 = 360 \div 5 = 72$.

- An interior angle of the hexagon measures 120, and an exterior angle measures 60.

- An interior angle of the pentagon measures 108, and an exterior angle measures 72.

Exercises

Sometimes regular octagons are pieced around a square to form a quilt pattern.

1. Classify $\angle 1$, $\angle 2$, $\angle 3$, and $\angle 4$ as interior or exterior angles.

2. Find the measures of $\angle 1$, $\angle 2$, $\angle 3$, and $\angle 4$.

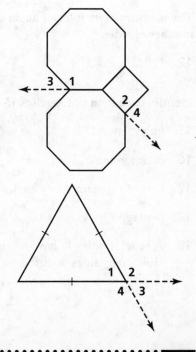

3. Classify $\angle 1$, $\angle 2$, $\angle 3$, and $\angle 4$ as interior angles, exterior angles, or neither.

4. Find the measures of $\angle 1$, $\angle 2$, $\angle 3$, and $\angle 4$.

Practice 3-4

Find the values of the variables for each polygon. Each is a regular polygon.

1.
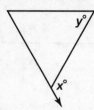

2.
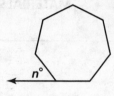

3.
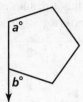

Find the missing angle measures.

4.
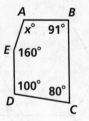

5.
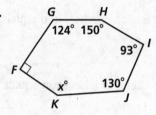

6.
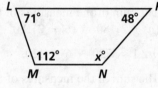

7.
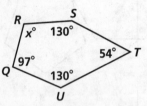

8.
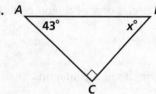

9.
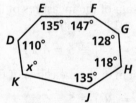

For a regular 12-sided polygon, find each of the following.

10. the measure of an exterior angle

11. the measure of an interior angle

The measure of an interior angle of a regular polygon is given. Find the number of sides.

12. 120

13. 108

14. 135

Identify each item in Exercises 15–18 in the figure.

15. quadrilateral

16. exterior angle

17. pair of supplementary angles

18. pentagon

19. A regular polygon has an exterior angle of measure 18. How many sides does the polygon have?

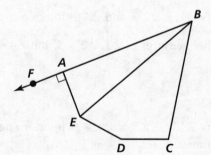

Reteaching 3-5

OBJECTIVE: Writing and graphing equations of lines

MATERIALS: Graphing paper

If you know two points on a line, or if you know one point and the slope of a line, then you can find the equation of the line.

Example

Write an equation of the line that contains the points $J(4, -5)$ and $K(-2, 1)$. Graph the line.

If you know two points on a line, first find the slope using $m = \frac{y_2 - y_1}{x_2 - x_1}$.

$$m = \frac{1 - (-5)}{-2 - 4} = \frac{6}{-6} = -1$$

Now you know two points and the slope of the line. Select one of the points to substitute for (x_1, y_1). Then find the equation using the point-slope form $y - y_1 = m(x - x_1)$.

$y - 1 = -1(x - (-2))$ Substitute.

$y - 1 = -1(x + 2)$ Simplify within parentheses. You may leave your equation in this form or further simplify to find the slope-intercept form.

$y - 1 = -x - 2$

$y = -x - 1$

Answer: Either $y - 1 = -1(x + 2)$ or $y = -x - 1$ is acceptable.

Exercises

Write an equation for the line with the given slope that contains the given point. Graph each line.

1. slope 2, $(2, -2)$

2. slope $\frac{1}{3}$, $(-6, -2)$

3. slope -1, $(-3, 0)$

4. slope $\frac{5}{6}$, $(-6, -3)$

5. slope $-\frac{1}{2}$, $(-4, 3)$

6. slope 0, $(3, 1)$

Write an equation for the line containing the given points. Graph each line.

7. $(2, 3), (4, -4)$

8. $(-4, 5), (3, -2)$

9. $(0, 1), (-5, -1)$

10. $(1, 1), (6, 1)$

11. $(-3, 0), (-5, 4)$

12. $(-3, 4), (-3, -1)$

Write an equation for the line with the given information. Graph each line.

13. contains point $(4, -2)$, slope -3

14. contains points $(3, -1), (5, 5)$

15. contains point $(2, 1)$, slope $\frac{1}{4}$

16. contains point $(8, -2)$, slope $-\frac{3}{4}$

17. contains points $(-4, 5), (-3, 4)$

18. contains points $(1, 1), (2, 1)$

Practice 3-5

Lines in the Coordinate Plane

Write an equation of the line with the given slope that contains the given point.

1. $F(3, -6)$, slope $\frac{1}{3}$

2. $Q(5, 2)$, slope -2

3. $A(3, 3)$, slope 7

4. $B(-4, -1)$, slope $-\frac{1}{2}$

5. $L(-3, -2)$, slope $\frac{1}{6}$

6. $R(15, 10)$, slope $\frac{4}{5}$

7. $D(1, -9)$, slope 4

8. $W(0, 6)$, slope -1

Graph each line using slope-intercept form.

9. $2y = 8x - 2$

10. $2y = \frac{1}{2}x - 10$

11. $3x + 9y = 18$

12. $-x + y = -1$

13. $y + 7 = 2x$

14. $4x - 2y = 6$

15. $5 - y = \frac{3}{4}x$

16. $\frac{1}{3}x = \frac{1}{2}y - 1$

Graph each line.

17. $y = 5x + 4$

18. $y = \frac{1}{2}x - 3$

19. $x = -2$

20. $y = -2x$

21. $y = -5$

22. $y = x$

23. $y = -\frac{2}{3}x + 2$

24. $x = 2.5$

Write an equation of the line containing the given points.

25. $A(2, 7), B(3, 4)$

26. $P(-1, 3), Q(0, 4)$

27. $S(10, 2), T(2, -2)$

28. $D(7, -4), E(-5, 2)$

29. $G(-2, 0), H(3, 10)$

30. $B(3, 5), C(-6, 2)$

31. $X(-1, -1), Y(4, -2)$

32. $M(8, -3), N(7, 3)$

Write equations for (a) the horizontal line and (b) the vertical line that contain the given point.

33. $Z(2, -11)$

34. $D(0, 2)$

35. $R(-4, -4)$

36. $F(-1, 8)$

Graph each line using intercepts.

37. $3x - y = 12$

38. $2x + 4y = -4$

39. $\frac{1}{2}x + \frac{1}{2}y = 3$

40. $12x - 3y = -6$

41. $2x - 2y = 8$

42. $\frac{1}{4}x + 2y = 2$

43. $-6x + 1.5y = 18$

44. $0.2x + 0.3y = 1.8$

45. The equation $P = \$3.90 + \$0.10x$ represents the hourly pay (P) a worker receives for loading x number of boxes onto a truck.

  a. What is the slope of the line represented by the given equation?

  b. What does the slope represent in this situation?

  c. What is the y-intercept of the line?

  d. What does the y-intercept represent in this situation?

46. The Blackberrys' driveway is difficult to get up in the winter ice and snow because of its slope. What is the equation of the line that represents the Blackberrys' driveway?

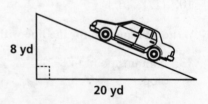

8 yd

20 yd

Reteaching 3-6

Slopes of Parallel and Perpendicular Lines

• •

OBJECTIVE: Identifying and writing equations for parallel and perpendicular lines	**MATERIALS:** Graphing paper

Example 1

Write an equation for the line that contains G (4, −3) and is parallel to $\overleftrightarrow{EF}$: $-\frac{1}{2}x + 2y = 6$. Write another equation for the line that contains G and is perpendicular to $\overleftrightarrow{EF}$. Graph the three lines.

Step 1 Rewrite in slope-intercept form: $y = \frac{1}{4}x + 3$

Step 2 Use point-slope form to write an equation for each line.

Parallel line: $m = \frac{1}{4}$	**Perpendicular line:** $m = -4$
$y - (-3) = \frac{1}{4}(x - 4)$	$y - (-3) = -4(x - 4)$
$y = \frac{1}{4}x - 4$	$y = -4x + 13$

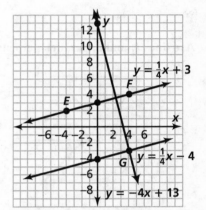

Example 2

Given points $J(-1, 4)$, $K(2, 3)$, $L(5, 4)$, and $M(0, -3)$, are $\overleftrightarrow{JK}$ and $\overleftrightarrow{LM}$ parallel, perpendicular, or neither?

$-\frac{1}{3} \neq \frac{7}{5}$ Their slopes are not equal, so they are not parallel.

$\frac{1}{3} \cdot \frac{7}{5} \neq -1$ The product of their slopes is not −1, so they are not perpendicular.

→ neither

Exercises

Find the slope of a line (a) parallel to and (b) perpendicular to each line.

1. $y = -2x$

2. $y = \frac{1}{4}x - 6$

3. $x = -3$

Write an equation for the line that (a) contains G and is parallel to $\overleftrightarrow{EF}$. Write another equation for the line that (b) contains G and is perpendicular to $\overleftrightarrow{EF}$. (c) Graph the three lines to check your answers.

4. $\overleftrightarrow{EF}$: $y = -2x + 5$, $G(1, 2)$ **5.** $\overleftrightarrow{EF}$: $6y + 4x = -12$, $G(0, -4)$ **6.** $\overleftrightarrow{EF}$: $x - \frac{1}{3}y = 4$, $G(-3, -2)$

Tell whether $\overleftrightarrow{JK}$ and $\overleftrightarrow{LM}$ are parallel, perpendicular, or neither.

7. $J(2, 0)$, $K(-1, 3)$, $L(0, 4)$, $M(-1, 5)$ **8.** $J(-4, -5)$, $K(5, 1)$, $L(6, 0)$, $M(4, 3)$

9.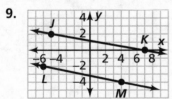

10.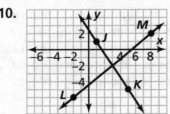

11.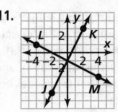

12. $\overleftrightarrow{JK}$: $y = \frac{1}{5}x + 2$
$\overleftrightarrow{LM}$: $y = 5x - \frac{1}{2}$

13. $\overleftrightarrow{JK}$: $2y + \frac{1}{2}x = -2$
$\overleftrightarrow{LM}$: $2x + 8y = 8$

14. $\overleftrightarrow{JK}$: $y = -1$
$\overleftrightarrow{LM}$: $x = 0$

• •

Practice 3-6

Slopes of Parallel and Perpendicular Lines

Are the lines parallel, perpendicular, or neither? Explain.

1. $y = 3x - 2$

$y = \frac{1}{3}x + 2$

2. $y = \frac{1}{2}x + 1$

$-4y = 8x + 3$

3. $\frac{2}{3}x + y = 4$

$y = -\frac{2}{3}x + 8$

4. $-x - y = -1$

$y + x = 7$

5. $y = 2$

$x = 0$

6. $3x + 6y = 30$

$4y + 2x = 9$

7. $y = x$

$8y - x = 8$

8. $\frac{1}{3}x + \frac{1}{2}y = 1$

$\frac{3}{4}y + \frac{1}{2}x = 1$

Are lines l_1 and l_2 parallel, perpendicular, or neither? Explain.

9.
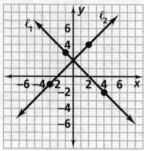

10.
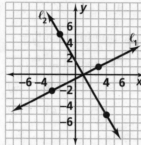

11.
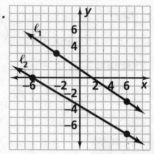

12.
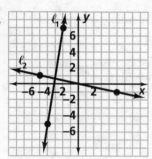

13.
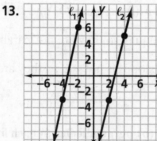

14.
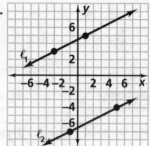

Write an equation for the line perpendicular to $\overleftrightarrow{XY}$ that contains point Z.

15. $\overleftrightarrow{XY}: 3x + 2y = -6, Z(3, 2)$

16. $\overleftrightarrow{XY}: y = \frac{3}{4}x + 22, Z(12, 8)$

17. $\overleftrightarrow{XY}: -x + y = 0, Z(-2, -1)$

Write an equation for the line parallel to $\overleftrightarrow{XY}$ that contains point Z.

18. $\overleftrightarrow{XY}: 6x - 10y + 5 = 0, Z(-5, 3)$

19. $\overleftrightarrow{XY}: y = -1, Z(0, 0)$

20. $\overleftrightarrow{XY}: x = \frac{1}{2}y + 1, Z(1, -2)$

21. Two planes are flying side by side at the same altitude. It is important that their paths do not intersect. One plane is flying along the path given by the line $4x - 2y = 10$. What is the slope-intercept form of the line that must be the path of another plane passing through the point $L(-1, -2)$ so that the planes do not collide? Graph the paths of the two planes.

Reteaching 3-7

Constructing Parallel and Perpendicular Lines

OBJECTIVE: Constructing perpendicular lines	**MATERIALS:** Straightedge, compass

Example

Construct a right triangle in which the lengths of the legs are *a* and *b*.

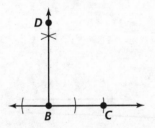

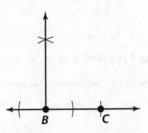

Step 1 Construct $\overline{BC}$ with length *a*.

Step 2 Construct a line perpendicular to $\overline{BC}$ through *B*.

Step 3 Construct point *D* on the perpendicular line so that $BD = b$.

Step 4 Draw $\overline{DC}$.

Exercises

Follow the given steps to construct a right triangle.

1. Construct a right triangle in which the length of one of the legs is *a* and the length of the hypotenuse is *b*. Use the following steps.

   Step 1 Construct $\overline{XY}$ with length *a*.

   Step 2 Construct a line perpendicular to $\overline{XY}$ through *X*.

   Step 3 Construct point *Z* on the perpendicular line so that $YZ = b$.

   Step 4 Draw $\overline{YZ}$.

For Exercises 2–4, use the lengths *a* and *b* given at the top of the page.

2. Construct a right triangle in which the length of each leg is *b*.

3. Construct a right triangle in which the length of one leg is *a* and the length of the hypotenuse is 2*a*.

4. Construct a right triangle in which the length of the hypotenuse is *b*.

Practice 3-7

Construct a line perpendicular to line *l* through point *Q*.

1.   •*Q*

2.   •*Q*

3.   •*Q*

ℓ

ℓ

ℓ

Construct a line perpendicular to line *l* at point *T*.

4. ◄———•———► *l*
          T

5. ◄———•———► *l*
          T

6. ◄———•———► *l*
          T

Construct a line parallel to line *l* and through point *K*.

7.   •*K*

8.   •*K*

9.   •*K*

ℓ

ℓ

ℓ

For Exercises 10–15, use the segments at the right.

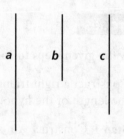

10. Construct a quadrilateral with one pair of parallel sides of lengths *a* and *b*.

11. Construct a quadrilateral with one pair of parallel sides of lengths *b* and *c*.

12. Construct a square with side lengths of *b*.

13. Construct a right triangle with leg lengths of *a* and *c*.

14. Construct a right triangle with leg lengths of *b* and *c*.

15. Construct an isosceles right triangle with leg lengths of *a*.

Reteaching 4-1

Congruent Figures and Corresponding Parts

· ·

OBJECTIVE: Recognizing congruent figures and their corresponding parts	**MATERIALS:** None

Example

$\triangle ABC \cong \triangle XYZ$. Find $m\angle A$.

Because the triangles are congruent, all corresponding parts are congruent.

Sides: $\overline{AB} \cong \overline{XY}$, $\overline{BC} \cong \overline{YZ}$, $\overline{AC} \cong \overline{XZ}$

Angles: $\angle A \cong \angle X$, $\angle B \cong \angle Y$, $\angle C \cong \angle Z$

Because $\angle B \cong \angle Y$, $m\angle B \cong 37$.

Use the Triangle Angle-Sum Theorem to find $m\angle A$.

$$m\angle A + m\angle B + m\angle C = 180$$
$$m\angle A + 37 + 63 = 180$$
$$m\angle A + 100 = 180$$
$$m\angle A = 80$$

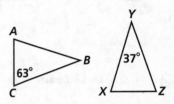

Exercises

Match each triangle in the first column with a congruent triangle in the second column.

1.

a.

2.

b.

3.

c.

Find the measure of the indicated angle.

4. $\triangle PQR \cong \triangle STU$. Find $m\angle U$.

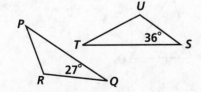

5. $EFGH \cong JKLM$. Find $m\angle M$.

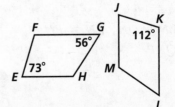

Practice 4-1

Congruent Figures and Corresponding Parts

Each pair of polygons is congruent. Find the measures of the numbered angles.

1. 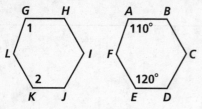   2. 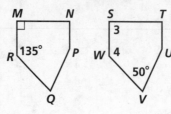   3.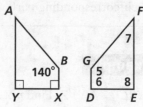

△*CAT* ≅ △*JSD*. **List each of the following.**

4. three pairs of congruent sides

5. three pairs of congruent angles

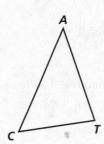

WXYZ ≅ *JKLM*. **List each of the following.**

6. four pairs of congruent sides

7. four pairs of congruent angles

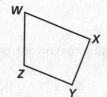

State whether the pairs of figures are congruent. Explain.

8. △*GHJ* and △*IHJ*

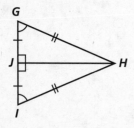

9. △*QRS* and △*TVS*

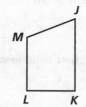

10. **Developing Proof** Use the information given in the diagram.
    Give a reason that each statement is true.

    a. ∠*L* ≅ ∠*Q*

    b. ∠*LNM* ≅ ∠*PNQ*

    c. ∠*M* ≅ ∠*P*

    d. $\overline{LM}$ ≅ $\overline{QP}$, $\overline{LN}$ ≅ $\overline{QN}$, $\overline{MN}$ ≅ $\overline{PN}$

    e. △*LNM* ≅ △*QNP*

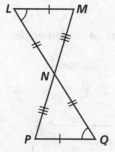

Geometry Chapter 4

Reteaching 4-2

OBJECTIVE: Proving two triangles congruent using the SSS and SAS postulates

MATERIALS: Ruler, protractor

Example

Name the triangle congruence postulate you can use to prove each pair of triangles congruent.

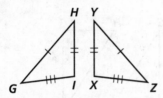

a. Because three sides of $\triangle GHI$ are congruent to three sides of $\triangle ZYX$, $\triangle GHI \cong \triangle ZYX$ by the SSS Postulate.

b. Because two sides and the included angle of $\triangle BCF$ are congruent to two sides and the included angle of $\triangle ECD$, $\triangle BCF \cong \triangle ECD$ by the SAS Postulate.

Exercises

Refer to the triangles at the right.

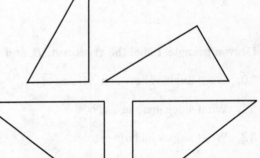

1. Use a ruler to show that the top two triangles at the right are congruent by the SSS Postulate.

2. Use a ruler and a protractor to show that the two large triangles at the right are congruent by the SAS Postulate.

Name the triangle congruence postulate you can use to prove each pair of triangles congruent. Then state the triangle congruence.

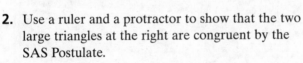

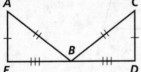 **3.**

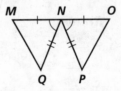 **4.**

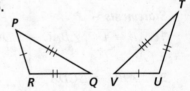 **5.**

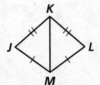 **6.**

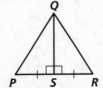 **7.**

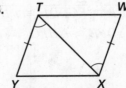 **8.**

Practice 4-2

Triangle Congruence by SSS and SAS

Decide whether you can use the SSS or SAS Postulate to prove the triangles congruent. If so, write the congruence statement, and identify the postulate. If not, write *not possible.*

1.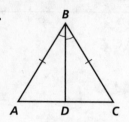

2.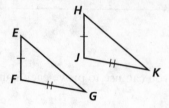

3.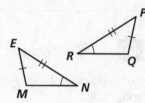

4.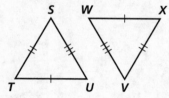

5.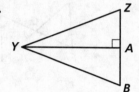

6.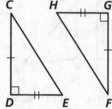

7.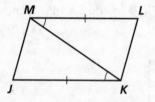

8.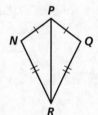

9.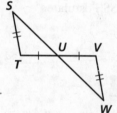

Draw a triangle. Label the vertices A, B, and C.

10. What angle is between $\overline{BC}$ and $\overline{AC}$?

11. What sides include $\angle B$?

12. What angles include $\overline{AB}$?

13. What side is included between $\angle A$ and $\angle C$?

14. **Developing Proof** Supply the reasons in this proof.

Given: $\overline{AB} \cong \overline{DC}$, $\angle BAC \cong \angle DCA$

Prove: $\triangle ABC \cong \triangle CDA$

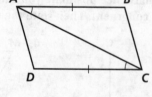

Statements	*Reasons*
1. $\overline{AB} \cong \overline{DC}$, $\angle BAC \cong \angle DCA$	a. ___?___
2. $\overline{AC} \cong \overline{CA}$	b. ___?___
3. $\triangle ABC \cong \triangle CDA$	c. ___?___

15. Write a proof.

Given: $\overline{EF} \cong \overline{FG}$, $\overline{DF} \cong \overline{FH}$

Prove: $\triangle DFE \cong \triangle HFG$

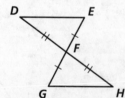

Reteaching 4-3

Triangle Congruence by AAS and ASA

OBJECTIVE: Proving two triangles congruent by the ASA Postulate and the AAS Theorem	MATERIALS: Ruler, protractor

Example

Tell whether the ASA Postulate or the AAS Theorem can be applied directly to prove the triangles congruent.

a. Because $\angle RDE$ and $\angle ADE$ are right angles, they are congruent. $\overline{ED} \cong \overline{ED}$ by the Reflexive Property of $\cong$, and it is given that $\angle R \cong \angle A$. Therefore, $\triangle RDE \cong \triangle ADE$ by the AAS Theorem.

b. It is given that $\overline{CH} \cong \overline{FH}$ and $\overline{EH} \cong \overline{BH}$. Because $\angle CHE$ and $\angle FHB$ are vertical angles, they are congruent. Therefore, $\triangle CHE \cong \triangle FHB$ by the ASA Postulate.

Exercises

Indicate congruences.

1. Copy the top figure at the right. Mark the figure with the angle congruence and side congruence symbols that you would need to prove the triangles congruent by the ASA Postulate.

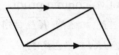

2. Copy the second figure shown. Mark the figure with the angle congruence and side congruence symbols that you would need to prove the triangles congruent by the AAS Theorem.

3. Draw two triangles that are congruent by either the ASA Postulate or the AAS Theorem.

What additional information would you need to prove each pair of triangles congruent by the stated postulate or theorem?

4. ASA

5. AAS

6. SAS

7. SSS

8. AAS

9. ASA

Practice 4-3

Tell whether the ASA Postulate or the AAS Theorem can be applied directly to prove the triangles congruent. If the triangles cannot be proved congruent, write *not possible*.

1.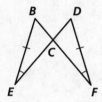

2.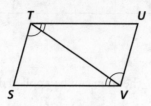

3.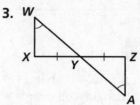

4.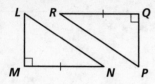

5.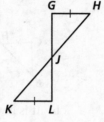

6.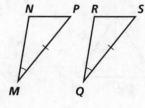

7.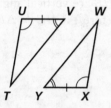

8.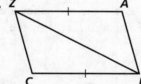

9.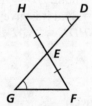

10. Write a two-column proof.
    Given: $\angle K \cong \angle M$, $\overline{KL} \cong \overline{ML}$
    Prove: $\triangle JKL \cong \triangle PML$

11. Write a flow proof.
    Given: $\angle Q \cong \angle S$, $\angle TRS \cong \angle RTQ$
    Prove: $\triangle QRT \cong \triangle STR$

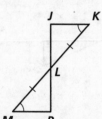

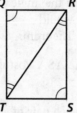

What else must you know to prove the triangles congruent for the reason shown?

12. ASA

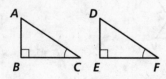

13. AAS

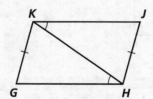

14. ASA

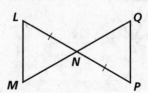

Reteaching 4-4

OBJECTIVE: Using triangle congruence and CPCTC to prove that the parts of two triangles are congruent

MATERIALS: None

Example

Write a two-column proof.

Given: $\overline{AB} \parallel \overline{DC}$, $\angle B \cong \angle D$
Prove: $\overline{BC} \cong \overline{DA}$

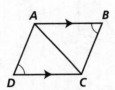

Statements	*Reasons*
1. $\overline{AB} \parallel \overline{DC}$	1. Given
2. $\angle BAC \cong \angle DCA$	2. If $\parallel$ lines, then alternate interior $\angle$s are $\cong$.
3. $\angle B \cong \angle D$	3. Given
4. $\overline{AC} \cong \overline{AC}$	4. Reflexive Property of $\cong$
5. $\triangle ABC \cong \triangle CDA$	5. AAS Theorem
6. $\overline{BC} \cong \overline{DA}$	6. CPCTC

Exercises

Complete the two-column proof.

1. Given: $\overline{QK} \cong \overline{QA}$; $\overrightarrow{QB}$ bisects $\angle KQA$
   Prove: $\overline{KB} \cong \overline{AB}$

Statements	*Reasons*
a. __?__	1. Given
2. $\angle KQB \cong \angle AQB$	b. __?__
c. __?__	3. Reflexive Property of $\cong$
4. $\triangle KBQ \cong \triangle ABQ$	d. __?__
5. $\overline{KB} \cong \overline{AB}$	e. __?__

Write a two-column proof.

2. Given: $\overline{MN} \cong \overline{MP}$, $\overline{NO} \cong \overline{PO}$
   Prove: $\angle N \cong \angle P$

3. Given: $\overline{ON}$ bisects $\angle JOH$, $\angle J \cong \angle H$
   Prove: $\overline{JN} \cong \overline{HN}$

Practice 4-4

Explain how you can use SSS, SAS, ASA, or AAS with CPCTC to prove each statement true.

1. $\angle A \cong \angle C$

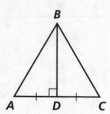

2. $\overline{HE} \cong \overline{FG}$

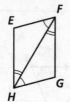

3. $\angle K \cong \angle P$

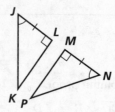

4. $\angle QST \cong \angle SQR$

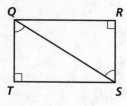

5. $\angle U \cong \angle W$

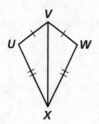

6. $\overline{ZA} \cong \overline{AC}$

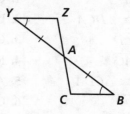

7. $\overline{FG} \cong \overline{DG}$

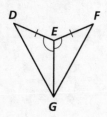

8. $\overline{JK} \cong \overline{KL}$

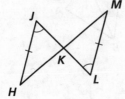

9. $\angle N \cong \angle Q$

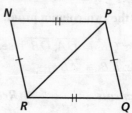

Write a Plan for Proof.

10. Given: $\overline{BD} \perp \overline{AB}, \overline{BD} \perp \overline{DE}, \overline{BC} \cong \overline{CD}$

Prove: $\angle A \cong \angle E$

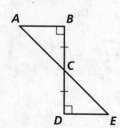

11. Given: $\overline{FJ} \cong \overline{GH}, \angle JFH \cong \angle GHF$

Prove: $\overline{FG} \cong \overline{JH}$

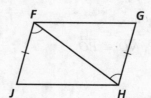

Reteaching 4-5

Isosceles and Equilateral Triangles

OBJECTIVE: Using and applying properties of isosceles triangles	**MATERIALS:** None

Example

Find $m\angle ABE$.

Because $AE \cong BE$, $m\angle EAB \cong m\angle ABE$.

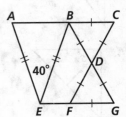

$m\angle EAB + m\angle ABE + m\angle AEB = 180$	Triangle Angle-Sum Theorem
$m\angle EAB + m\angle ABE + 40 = 180$	Substitution
$m\angle EAB + m\angle ABE = 140$	Subtraction Property of Equality
$2m\angle ABE = 140$	Substitution
$m\angle ABE = 70$	Division Property of Equality

Exercises

Work with a partner to find the measures of the angles of quadrilateral *BDFE* in the diagram above.

1. Find the measures of the angles of $\triangle CBD$ and $\triangle FDG$.

2. Use the Angle Addition Postulate to find $m\angle BDF$.

3. Use the Angle Addition Postulate to find $m\angle EFC$.

4. Use the Angle Addition Postulate to find $m\angle EBG$.

5. Use the Polygon Interior Angle-Sum Theorem to find $m\angle BEF$.

Find the measure of each angle.

6. $m\angle BCA$

7. $m\angle DCE$

8. $m\angle DEF$

9. $m\angle BCD$

10. $m\angle BAG$

11. $m\angle GAH$

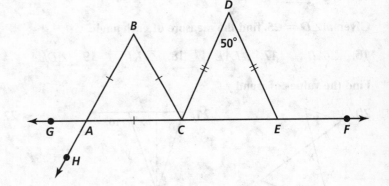

Practice 4-5

Isosceles and Equilateral Triangles

Find the values of the variables.

1.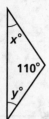

2.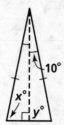

3.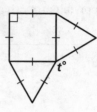

4.

5.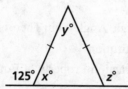

6. *WXYZV* is a regular polygon.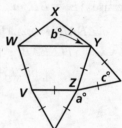

7.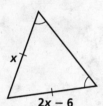

8.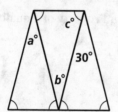

9.

Complete each statement. Explain why it is true.

10. $\overline{AF} \cong$ _?_

11. $\overline{CA} \cong$ _?_

12. $\overline{KI} \cong$ _?_

13. $\overline{EC} \cong$ _?_

14. $\overline{JA} \cong$ _?_

15. $\overline{HB} \cong$ _?_

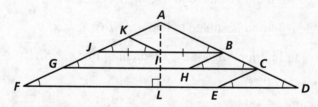

Given $m\angle D = 25$, **find the measure of each angle.**

16. $\angle JAB$ **17.** $\angle FAL$ **18.** $\angle JKI$ **19.** $\angle DLA$

Find the values of *x* and *y*.

20.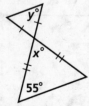

21.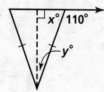

22.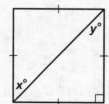

Reteaching 4-6

Congruence in Right Triangles

• •

OBJECTIVE: Proving triangles congruent by the HL Theorem	**MATERIALS:** Ruler

Example

Explain why $\triangle GFD \cong \triangle EFD$ by the HL Theorem.

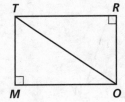

To prove two triangles congruent by the HL Theorem, prove that:

1. They are right triangles.

1. $\angle GFD$ and $\angle EFD$ are right angles. Therefore, $\triangle GFD$ and $\triangle EFD$ are right triangles.

2. Their hypotenuses are congruent.

2. $\overline{GD} \cong \overline{ED}$ is given.

3. One pair of legs is $\cong$.

3. $\overline{DF} \cong \overline{DF}$ by the Reflexive Property of $\cong$.

Exercises

Measure the hypotenuses and the length of one pair of legs to decide whether the triangles are congruent by the HL Theorem. If the triangles are congruent, state the congruence.

1.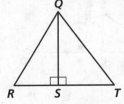

2.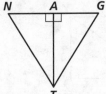

3.

Tell whether the HL Theorem can be applied to prove the triangles congruent. If possible, write the triangle congruence.

4.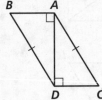

5.

6.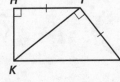

7.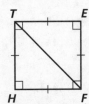

8.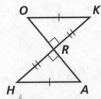

9.

Practice 4-6

Congruence in Right Triangles

Write a two-column proof.

1. Given: $\overline{AB} \perp \overline{BC}$, $\overline{ED} \perp \overline{FE}$, $\overline{AB} \cong \overline{ED}$, $\overline{AC} \cong \overline{FD}$
Prove: $\triangle ABC \cong \triangle DEF$

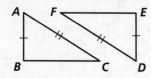

2. Given: $\angle P$ and $\angle R$ are right angles, $\overline{PS} \cong \overline{QR}$
Prove: $\triangle PQS \cong \triangle RSQ$

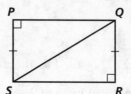

Write a flow proof.

3. Given: $\overline{MJ} \perp \overline{NK}$, $\overline{MN} \cong \overline{MK}$
Prove: $\triangle MJN \cong \triangle MJK$

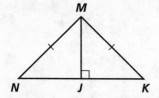

4. Given: $\overline{GI} \cong \overline{JI}$, $\angle GHI \cong \angle JHI$
Prove: $\triangle IHG \cong \triangle IHJ$

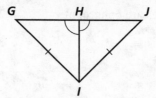

What additional information do you need to prove each pair of triangles congruent by the HL Theorem?

5.

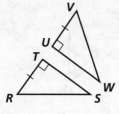

6.

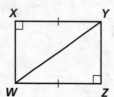

7.

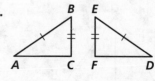

8.

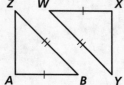

9.

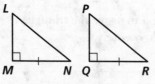

10.

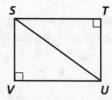

11.

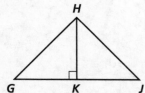

12.

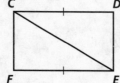

13.

Reteaching 4-7

Using Corresponding Parts of Congruent Triangles

OBJECTIVE: Proving triangles congruent by first proving two other triangles congruent	**MATERIALS:** None

Sometimes you can prove one pair of triangles congruent and then use corresponding parts of those triangles to prove another pair congruent.

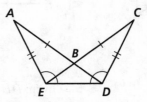

Example

Write a paragraph proof.

Given: $\overline{AB} \cong \overline{CB}$, $\overline{AE} \cong \overline{CD}$, $\angle AED \cong \angle CDE$

Prove: $\triangle ABE \cong \triangle CBD$

$\overline{ED} \cong \overline{ED}$ by the Reflexive Property of $\cong$. It is given that $\overline{AE} \cong \overline{CD}$ and $\triangle AED \cong \triangle CDE$. Therefore, $\triangle AED \cong \triangle CDE$ by the SAS Postulate. $\angle A \cong \angle C$ by CPCTC. It is given that $\overline{AB} \cong \overline{CB}$. Therefore, $\triangle ABE \cong \triangle CBD$ by the SAS Postulate.

Exercises

Use the Plan for Proof to write a two-column proof.

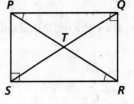

1. Given: $\angle PSR$ and $\angle PQR$ are right angles, $\angle QPR \cong \angle SRP$

   Prove: $\triangle STR \cong \triangle QTP$

   Plan for Proof: Prove $\triangle QPR \cong \triangle SRP$ by the AAS Theorem. Then use CPCTC and vertical angles to prove $\triangle STR \cong \triangle QTP$ by the AAS Theorem.

Write a Plan for Proof.

2. Given: $\angle MLP \cong \angle QPL$, $\angle M \cong \angle Q$

   Prove: $\triangle MLN \cong \triangle QPN$

3. Given: $\overline{AB} \cong \overline{ED}$, $\overline{BC} \cong \overline{DC}$

   Prove: $\triangle ABF \cong \triangle EDF$

Practice 4-7

Using Corresponding Parts of Congruent Triangles

Name a pair of overlapping congruent triangles in each diagram. State whether the triangles are congruent by SSS, SAS, ASA, AAS, or HL.

1. Given: $\overline{ZW} \cong \overline{XY}$, $\angle YXW$ and $\angle ZWX$ are right $\angle$s

2. Given: $\angle ABC \cong \angle DCB$, $\angle CBD \cong \angle BCA$

3. Given: $\overline{EJ} \parallel \overline{FK}$, $\overline{GJ} \parallel \overline{HK}$, $\overline{EG} \cong \overline{HF}$

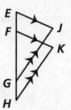

4. Given: $\overline{LP} \cong \overline{LO}$, $\overline{PM} \cong \overline{ON}$

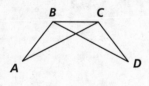

5. Given: $\overline{DE} \cong \overline{FG}$, $\overline{AC} \cong \overline{CB}$, $\overline{EC} \cong \overline{FC}$

6. Given: $\angle YUV \cong \angle XVU$, $\angle WUV \cong \angle WVU$

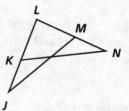

Separate and redraw the indicated triangles. Identify any common angles or sides.

7. △ABC and △DCB

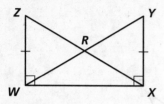

8. △EFG and △HGF

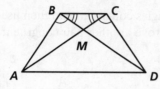

9. △JML and △NKL

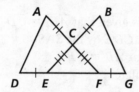

Write a two-column proof, a paragraph proof, or a flow proof.

10. Given: $\overline{AX} \cong \overline{AY}$, $\overline{CX} \perp \overline{AB}$, $\overline{BY} \perp \overline{AC}$
Prove: △BYA ≅ △CXA

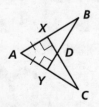

11. Given: $\overline{FH} \cong \overline{GE}$, $\angle HFG \cong \angle EGF$
Prove: △GEH ≅ △FHE

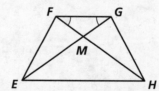

Reteaching 5-1

OBJECTIVE: Using properties of midsegments to solve problems

MATERIALS: Ruler

Example

$\overline{DE}$ is the midsegment of $\triangle ABC$. $\overline{FG}$ is the midsegment of $\triangle ADE$. $\overline{HI}$ is the midsegment of $\triangle AFG$. If $BC = 12$, find DE, FG, and HI.

$$DE = \frac{1}{2}BC \qquad FG = \frac{1}{2}DE \qquad HI = \frac{1}{2}FG$$

$$= \frac{1}{2}(12) \qquad\quad = \frac{1}{2}(6) \qquad\quad = \frac{1}{2}(3)$$

$$= 6 \qquad\qquad\quad = 3 \qquad\qquad = 1.5$$

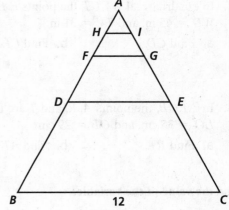

Exercises

Follow the indicated steps to complete each exercise.

- Draw a triangle. Label it $\triangle XYZ$.

- Draw the midsegment of $\triangle XYZ$ parallel to $\overline{YZ}$. Label it $\overline{MN}$.

- Draw the midsegment of $\triangle XMN$ parallel to $\overline{MN}$. Label it $\overline{PQ}$.

- Draw the midsegment of $\triangle XPQ$ parallel to $\overline{PQ}$. Label it $\overline{RS}$.

    1. If $RS = 4$, find the following lengths.

        a. PQ **b.** MN **c.** YZ

- Draw a triangle. Label it $\triangle PUV$.

- Draw the midsegment of $\triangle PUV$ parallel to $\overline{UV}$. Label it $\overline{ST}$.

- Draw the midsegment of $\triangle PST$ parallel to $\overline{ST}$. Label it $\overline{QR}$.

- Draw the midsegment of $\triangle PQR$ parallel to $\overline{QR}$. Label it $\overline{NO}$.

    2. If $QR = 5$, find the following lengths.

        a. NO **b.** ST **c.** UV

    3. If $NO = 2$, find the following lengths.

        a. QR **b.** ST **c.** UV

Practice 5-1

Use the diagrams at the right to complete the exercises.

1. In $\triangle MNO$, the points C, D, and E are midpoints. $CD = 4$ cm, $CE = 8$ cm, and $DE = 7$ cm.

   a. Find MO.　　　**b.** Find NO.　　　**c.** Find MN.

2. In quadrilateral $WVUT$, the points F, E, D, and C are midpoints. $WU = 45$ in. and $TV = 31$ in.

   a. Find CD.　　　**b.** Find CF.　　　**c.** Find ED.

3. In $\triangle LOB$, the points A, R, and T are midpoints. $LB = 19$ cm, $LO = 35$ cm, and $OB = 29$ cm.

   a. Find RT.　　　**b.** Find AT.　　　**c.** Find AR.

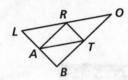

Find the value of the variable.

4.

5.
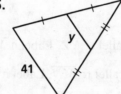

6.

7. Perimeter of $\triangle ABC = 32$ cm

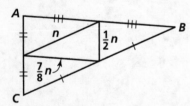

8.
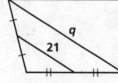

9.

10. $\overline{QR}$ is a midsegment of $\triangle LMN$.

   a. $QR = 9$. Find NM.

   b. $LN = 12$ and $LM = 31$. Find the perimeter of $\triangle LMN$.

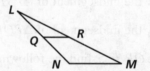

Use the given measures to identify three pairs of parallel segments in each diagram.

11.
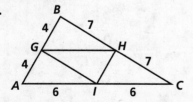

12.
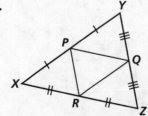

Reteaching 5-2

OBJECTIVE: Determining whether a given point lies on the perpendicular bisector of a segment

MATERIALS: Graph paper

Example

Given points $A(1, 3)$, $B(5, 1)$, and $C(4, 4)$, does C lie on the perpendicular bisector of $\overline{AB}$?

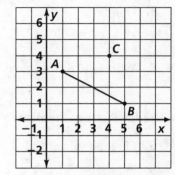

Plot the points on a coordinate grid. Draw $\overline{AB}$.
Use the distance formula to determine whether $AC = BC$.

$$AC = \sqrt{(1 - 4)^2 + (3 - 4)^2} \qquad BC = \sqrt{(5 - 4)^2 + (1 - 4)^2}$$

$$AC = \sqrt{(-3)^2 + (-1)^2} \qquad BC = \sqrt{1^2 + (-3)^2}$$

$$AC = \sqrt{9 + 1} \qquad BC = \sqrt{1 + 9}$$

$$AC = \sqrt{10} \qquad BC = \sqrt{10}$$

Because $AC = \sqrt{10}$ and $BC = \sqrt{10}$, $AC = BC$, and C lies on the perpendicular bisector of $\overline{AB}$.

Exercises

Complete these exercises on bisectors.

1. Given $D(3, 1)$, $E(7, 2)$, and $F(4, 5)$, does F lie on the perpendicular bisector of $\overline{DE}$?

2. Given $X(1, 2)$, $Y(7, 2)$, and $Z(4, 6)$, does Z lie on the perpendicular bisector of $\overline{XY}$?

3. Given $H(-4, 5)$, $I(-6, 2)$, and $J(-1, 3)$, does H lie on the perpendicular bisector of $\overline{IJ}$?

4. Given $P(-7, -7)$, $Q(-5, -2)$, and $R(0, -5)$, does Q lie on the perpendicular bisector of $\overline{PR}$?

5. Point $T(-9, 5)$ lies on the perpendicular bisector of $\overline{UV}$. If the coordinates of point U are $(-2, 1)$, which of the following are the coordinates of point V?

   A. $(-2, 7)$ **B.** $(-1, 6)$ **C.** $(0, 5)$

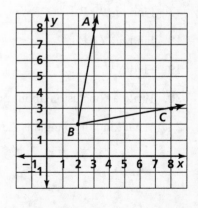

6. Use the diagram at the right. Which of the following points lies on the angle bisector of $\angle ABC$?

   A. $(6, 5)$ **B.** $(7, 8)$ **C.** $(4, 4)$

Practice 5-2

Bisectors in Triangles

Use the figure at the right for Exercises 1–5.

1. How is $\overline{WY}$ related to $\overline{XZ}$?

2. Find *XV*.

3. Find *WZ*.

4. Find *XY*.

5. What kind of triangle is $\triangle WXV$?

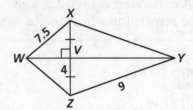

Use the figure at the right for Exercises 6–10.

6. Find the value of *x*.

7. Find *HI*.

8. Find *JI*.

9. If *L* lies on $\overline{KI}$, then *L* is ___?___ from *H* and *J*.

10. What kind of triangle is $\triangle HIJ$?

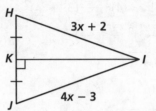

Use the figure at the right for Exercises 11–14.

11. Find the value of *y*.

12. Find *PS*.

13. Find *RS*.

14. What kind of triangle is $\triangle PQS$?

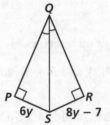

Use the figure at the right for Exercises 15–21.

15. How is $\overrightarrow{JP}$ related to $\angle LJN$?

16. Find the value of *x*.

17. Find $m\angle KJP$.

18. Find $m\angle OJP$.

19. Find *NM*.

20. Write a conclusion about point *M*.

21. What kind of triangle is $\triangle JOP$?

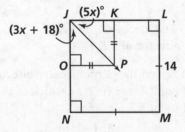

Reteaching 5-3

Concurrent Lines, Medians, and Altitudes

OBJECTIVE: Finding the point of concurrency of the altitudes of acute, obtuse, and right triangles

MATERIALS: Protractor, straightedge

Example

Draw an obtuse triangle. Find the point of concurrency of the lines containing its altitudes.

Draw obtuse triangle ABC.

Extend side $\overline{AB}$.

Move the straightedge on your protractor along $\overrightarrow{AB}$ until C lies directly under 90. Label the point lying directly under C on $\overrightarrow{AB}$ as point D.

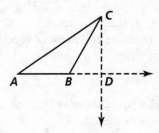

Draw $\overrightarrow{CD}$, the ray containing the altitude $\overline{CD}$.

Extend side $\overline{BC}$.

Move the straightedge on your protractor along $\overrightarrow{CB}$ until point A lies directly under 90. Label the point lying directly under A on $\overrightarrow{CB}$ as point E.

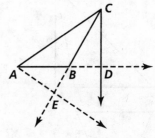

Draw $\overrightarrow{AE}$, the ray containing the altitude $\overline{AE}$.

Move the straightedge on your protractor along $\overrightarrow{AC}$ until B lies directly under 90. Label the point directly under B on $\overrightarrow{AC}$ as point F.

Draw $\overrightarrow{FB}$, the ray containing the altitude $\overline{BF}$.

The point of concurrency is G.

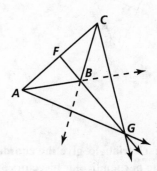

Exercises

Determine the point of concurrency.

1. Draw an acute triangle. Find the point of concurrency of the lines containing its altitudes.

2. Draw a right triangle. Find the point of concurrency of the lines containing its altitudes.

Practice 5-3

Concurrent Lines, Medians, and Altitudes

• •

Find the center of the circle that circumscribes △LMN.

1.
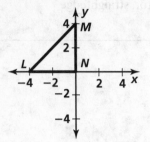

2.
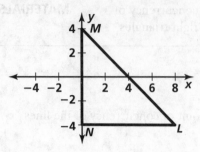

3.
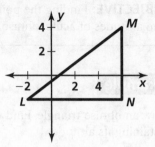

4. Construct the angle bisectors for △ABC.
Then use the point of concurrency to construct an inscribed circle.

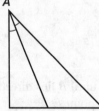

Is $\overline{AB}$ a perpendicular bisector, an angle bisector, an altitude, a median, or none of these?

5.
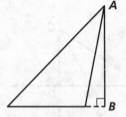

6.
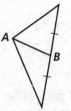

7.
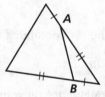

8.

9.

10.

For each triangle, give the coordinates of the point of concurrency of (a) the perpendicular bisectors of the sides and (b) the altitudes.

11.
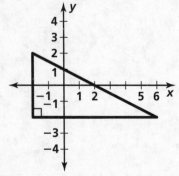

12.
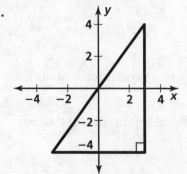

13.
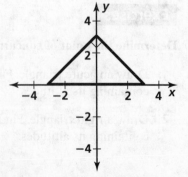

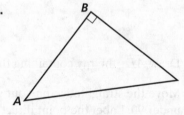

Reteaching 5-4

Inverses, Contrapositives, and Indirect Reasoning

OBJECTIVE: Writing convincing arguments using indirect reasoning	**MATERIALS:** None

Example

Given: $\angle A$ and $\angle B$ are not complementary.

Prove: $\angle C$ is not a right angle.

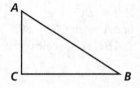

Step 1: Assume that $\angle C$ is a right angle.

Step 2: If $\angle C$ is a right angle, then by the Triangle Angle-Sum Theorem
$m\angle A + m\angle B + 90 = 180$. So $m\angle A + m\angle B = 90$. Therefore, $\angle A$ and $\angle B$ are complementary. But $\angle A$ and $\angle B$ are not complementary.

Step 3: Therefore, $\angle C$ is not a right angle.

Exercises

Complete the proofs.

1. Arrange the statements given at the right to complete the steps of the indirect proof.

   Given: $\overline{XY} \not\cong \overline{YZ}$

   Prove: $\angle 1 \not\cong \angle 4$

   Step 1: _?_
   Step 2: _?_
   Step 3: _?_
   Step 4: _?_
   Step 5: _?_
   Step 6: _?_

   A. But $\overline{XY} \not\cong \overline{YZ}$.

   B. Assume $\angle 1 \cong \angle 4$.

   C. Therefore, $\angle 1 \not\cong \angle 4$.

   D. $\angle 1$ and $\angle 2$ are supplementary, and $\angle 3$ and $\angle 4$ are supplementary.

   E. According to the Converse of the Isosceles Triangle Theorem, $XY = YZ$ or $\overline{XY} \cong \overline{YZ}$.

   F. If $\angle 1 \cong \angle 4$, then by the Congruent Supplements Theorem, $\angle 2 \cong \angle 3$.

2. Complete the steps below to write a convincing argument using indirect reasoning.

   Given: $\triangle DEF$ with $\angle D \not\cong \angle F$

   Prove: $\overline{EF} \not\cong \overline{DE}$

   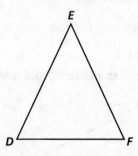

   Step 1: _?_
   Step 2: _?_
   Step 3: _?_
   Step 4: _?_

Practice 5-4

Inverses, Contrapositives, and Indirect Reasoning

Identify the two statements that contradict each other.

1. I. $ABCD$ is a trapezoid.
    II. $\overline{AB} \parallel \overline{CD}$
    III. $\overline{BC} \parallel \overline{AD}$

2. I. $\overline{AB} \cong \overline{BC}$
    II. $m\angle A + m\angle B = 80$
    III. $\triangle ABC$ is isosceles.

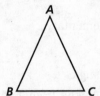

Write the negation of each statement.

3. The angle measure is 65.

4. Tina has her driver's license.

5. The figure has eight sides.

6. The restaurant is not open on Sunday.

7. $\triangle ABC$ is not congruent to $\triangle XYZ$.

8. $m\angle Y > 50$

Write (a) the inverse and (b) the contrapositive of each statement. Give the truth value of each.

9. If two triangles are congruent, then their corresponding angles are congruent.

10. If you live in Toronto, then you live in Canada.

Write the first step of an indirect proof.

11. $m\angle A = m\angle B$

12. $TUVW$ is a trapezoid.

13. $\overline{LM}$ intersects $\overline{NO}$.

14. $\triangle FGH$ is equilateral.

15. It is sunny outside.

16. $\angle D$ is not obtuse.

17. Write an indirect proof that $m\angle A < 90$.

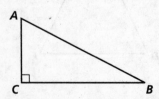

Reteaching 5-5

OBJECTIVE: Using inequalities involving triangle side lengths and angle measures to solve problems

MATERIALS: Straightedge

Example

Use the triangle inequality theorems to answer the questions.

a. Which is the largest angle of $\triangle ABC$?
$\overline{AB}$ is the longest side of $\triangle ABC$.
$\angle C$ lies opposite $\overline{AB}$.
$\angle C$ is the largest angle of $\triangle ABC$.

b. Which is the shortest side of $\triangle DEF$?
Find $m\angle E$.

$m\angle D + m\angle E + m\angle F = 180$	Triangle Angle-Sum Theorem
$30 + m\angle E + 90 = 180$	Substitution
$120 + m\angle E = 180$	Addition
$m\angle E = 60$	Subtraction Property of Equality

$\angle D$ is the smallest angle of $\triangle DEF$.
Because $\overline{FE}$ lies opposite $\angle D$,
$\overline{FE}$ is the shortest side of $\triangle DEF$.

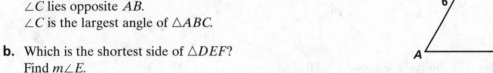

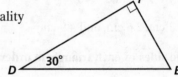

Exercises

Complete the following exercises.

1. Draw three triangles, one obtuse, one acute, and one right. Label the vertices. Exchange your triangles with a partner.

   a. Identify the longest and shortest sides of each triangle.

   b. Identify the largest and smallest angles of each triangle.

   c. Describe the relationship between the longest and shortest sides and the largest and smallest angles for each of your partner's triangles.

Which are the largest and smallest angles of each triangle?

2.

3.

4.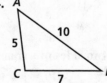

Which are the longest and shortest sides of each triangle?

5.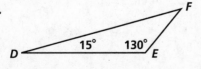

6.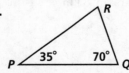

7.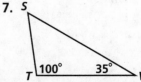

Name _____ Class _____ Date _____

Practice 5-5

Inequalities in Triangles

● ●

Determine the two largest angles in each triangle.

1.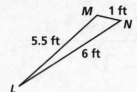

2.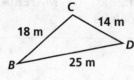

3.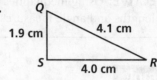

4.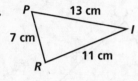

5.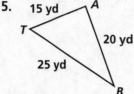

6.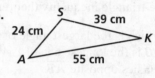

Can a triangle have sides with the given lengths? Explain.

7. 4 m, 7 m, and 8 m

8. 6 m, 10 m, and 17 m

9. 4 in., 4 in., and 4 in.

10. 1 yd, 9 yd, and 9 yd

11. 11 m, 12 m, and 13 m

12. 18 ft, 20 ft, and 40 ft

13. 1.2 cm, 2.6 cm, and 4.9 cm

14. $8\frac{1}{2}$ yd, $9\frac{1}{4}$ yd, and 18 yd

15. 2.5 m, 3.5 m, and 6 m

List the sides of each triangle in order from shortest to longest.

16.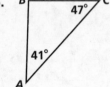

17.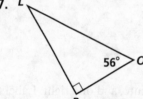

18.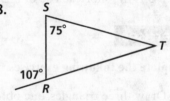

List the angles of each triangle in order from largest to smallest.

19.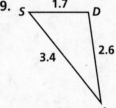

20.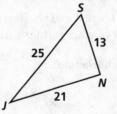

21.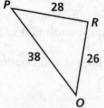

The lengths of two sides of a triangle are given. Describe the lengths possible for the third side.

22. 4 in., 7 in.

23. 9 cm, 17 cm

24. 5 ft, 5 ft

25. 11 m, 20 m

26. 6 km, 8 km

27. 24 in., 37 in.

Reteaching 6-1

OBJECTIVE: Classifying special types of quadrilaterals

MATERIALS: Ruler, protractor

quadrilateral   parallelogram   rhombus   rectangle   square   kite   trapezoid   isosceles trapezoid

Example

Judging by appearance, name *WXYZ* in as many ways as possible.

It is a quadrilateral because it has four sides.

It is a parallelogram because both pairs of opposite sides are parallel.

It is a rhombus because it has four congruent sides.

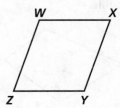

Exercises

Use a protractor and a ruler to sketch an example of each quadrilateral. Then name it in as many ways as possible.

1. a quadrilateral with exactly one pair of parallel sides

2. a quadrilateral with opposite sides parallel

3. a quadrilateral with four right angles

4. a quadrilateral with four congruent sides

Classify each quadrilateral by its most precise name.

5.

6.

7.

8.

9.

10.

11.

12.

Practice 6-1

Classifying Quadrilaterals

Determine the most precise name for each quadrilateral.

1.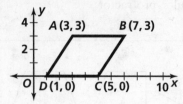

2.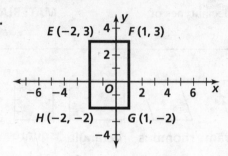

Judging by appearance, classify each quadrilateral in as many ways as possible.

3.

4.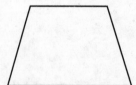

5.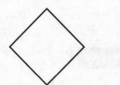

6.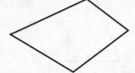

7.

8.

Algebra **Find the values of the variables. Then find the lengths of the sides of each quadrilateral.**

9. rhombus *ABDC*

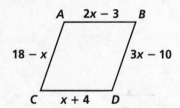

10. parallelogram *LONM*

11. square *FGHI*

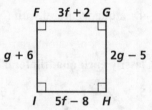

Determine the most precise name for each quadrilateral with the given vertices.

12. $A(1, 4), B(3, 5), C(6, 1), D(4, 0)$

13. $W(0, 5), X(3, 5), Y(3, 1), Z(0, 1)$

14. $A(-2, 4), B(2, 6), C(6, 4), D(2, -3)$

15. $P(-1, 0), Q(-1, 3), R(2, 4), S(2, 1)$

Reteaching 6-2

OBJECTIVE: Finding relationships among angles, sides, and diagonals of parallelograms	MATERIALS: None

Example

Use a two-column proof to prove Theorem 6-2: Opposite angles of a parallelogram are congruent.

Given: parallelogram $ABCD$

Prove: $\angle B \cong \angle D$

Statements	*Reasons*
1. parallelogram $ABCD$	1. Given
2. $\overline{AB} \cong \overline{CD}$, $\overline{BC} \cong \overline{DA}$	2. Opposite sides of a parallelogram are congruent.
3. $\overline{AC} \cong \overline{CA}$	3. Reflexive Property
4. $\triangle ABC \cong \triangle CDA$	4. SSS
5. $\angle B \cong \angle D$	5. CPCTC

Exercises

Use the figure to write a proof for each.

1. The proof in the example demonstrates that one pair of opposite angles is congruent. Prove that the other pair of opposite angles is congruent in parallelogram $ABCD$ above.

2. Given: parallelogram $ACDE$;
   $\overline{CD} \cong \overline{BD}$

   Prove: $\angle CBD \cong \angle E$

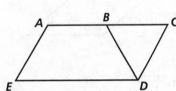

3. Given: parallelogram $ACDE$;
   $\overline{AE} \cong \overline{BD}$

   Prove: $\angle CBD \cong \angle C$

4. Given: parallelogram $ACDE$;
   $\angle CBD \cong \angle E$

   Prove: $\triangle BDC$ is isosceles.

5. Given: isosceles trapezoid $ABDE$;
   $\angle C \cong \angle E$

   Prove: $\overline{AE} \cong \overline{CD}$

Practice 6-2

Find the value of *x* in each parallelogram.

1.

2.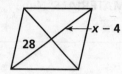

3.

4.

5. *AC* = 24

6.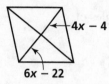

7. *x* = *EG*

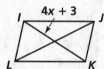

8. *IK* = 35

If *AE* = 17 and *BF* = 18, find the measures of the sides of parallelogram *BNXL*.

9. *BN*

10. *NX*

11. *XL*

12. *BL*

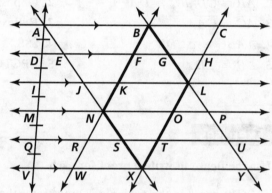

Find the measures of the numbered angles for each parallelogram.

13.

14.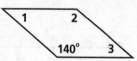

15.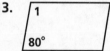

16.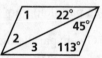

17.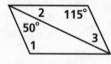

18.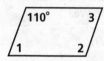

19.

20.

Find the length of $\overline{TI}$ in each parallelogram.

21.

22. $OR = \frac{7}{8}IO$

23. *TR* = 14, *ME* = 31

24. *IE* = 6, *GT* = 8

Name _____ Class _____ Date _____

Reteaching 6-3

Proving That a Quadrilateral Is a Parallelogram

OBJECTIVE: Finding characteristics of quadrilaterals that indicate that the quadrilaterals are parallelograms	**MATERIALS:** None

Example

Use a two-column proof to prove Theorem 6-6: If one pair of opposite sides of a quadrilateral is both congruent and parallel, then the quadrilateral is a parallelogram.

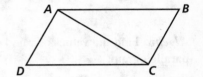

Given: quadrilateral $ABCD$

$\overline{AB} \cong \overline{CD}$

$\overline{AB} \parallel \overline{CD}$

Prove: $ABCD$ is a parallelogram.

Statements	*Reasons*
1. quadrilateral $ABCD$, $\overline{AB} \cong \overline{CD}$, $\overline{AB} \parallel \overline{CD}$	1. Given
2. $\angle BAC \cong \angle DCA$	2. Parallel lines form congruent alternate interior angles.
3. $\overline{AC} \cong \overline{CA}$	3. Reflexive Property
4. $\triangle ABC \cong \triangle CDA$	4. SAS
5. $\angle DAC \cong \angle BCA$	5. CPCTC
6. $\overline{AD} \parallel \overline{CB}$	6. If alternate interior angles are congruent, then lines are parallel.
7. $ABCD$ is a parallelogram.	7. Definition of parallelogram

Exercises

Determine whether the given information is sufficient to prove that quadrilateral *WXYZ* is a parallelogram.

1. $\overline{WY}$ bisects $\overline{ZX}$

2. $\overline{WX} \parallel \overline{ZY}$; $\overline{WZ} \cong \overline{XY}$

3. $\overline{VZ} \cong \overline{VX}$; $\overline{WX} \cong \overline{ZY}$

4. $\angle VWZ \cong \angle VYX$; $\overline{WZ} \cong \overline{XY}$

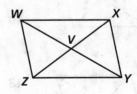

Use the figure at the right to complete each proof.

5. Given: triangle with $\overline{BD} \cong \overline{CD}$, $\overline{AE} \cong \overline{BD}$, and $\overline{AE} \parallel \overline{CD}$

   Prove: $ACDE$ is a parallelogram.

6. Given: $\angle CBD \cong \angle C$, $\overline{AE} \cong \overline{BD}$, and $\overline{AC} \cong \overline{ED}$

   Prove: $ACDE$ is a parallelogram.

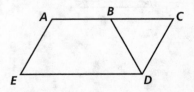

Practice 6-3

Proving That a Quadrilateral Is a Parallelogram

State whether the information given about quadrilateral *SMTP* is sufficient to determine that it is a parallelogram.

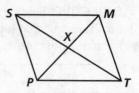

1. $\angle SPT \cong \angle SMT$

2. $\angle SPX \cong \angle TMX, \angle TPX \cong \angle SMX$

3. $\overline{SM} \cong \overline{PT}, \overline{SP} \cong \overline{MT}$

4. $\overline{SX} \cong \overline{XT}, \overline{SM} \cong \overline{PT}$

5. $\overline{PX} \cong \overline{MX}, \overline{SX} \cong \overline{TX}$

6. $\overline{SP} \cong \overline{MT}, \overline{SP} \parallel \overline{MT}$

Algebra Find the values of *x* and *y* for which the figure must be a parallelogram.

7.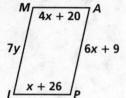

8.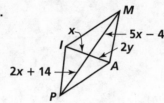

9.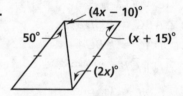

Algebra Find the value of *x*. Then tell whether the figure must be a parallelogram. Explain your answer.

10.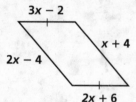

11.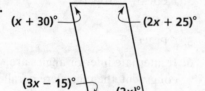

12. Given with angles $(4x - 10)°$, $(x + 15)°$, $50°$, $(2x)°$

Decide whether the quadrilateral is a parallelogram. Explain your answer.

13.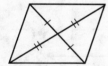

14.

15.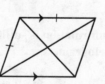

16.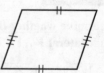

17.

18.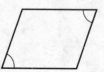

19.

20.

Reteaching 6-4

OBJECTIVE: Finding properties of rectangles and rhombuses

MATERIALS: None

Example

Find the measures of the numbered angles in the rectangle.

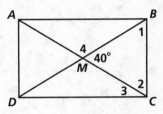

Because $\angle 4$ and $\angle BMC$ are supplementary, $m\angle 4 = 140$.

Because the diagonals of a rectangle are congruent, $AC = BD$. And because the diagonals bisect each other, $BM = CM$. Therefore, $\triangle BMC$ is isosceles with $BM = CM$.

So, by the Isosceles Triangle Theorem, $m\angle 1 = m\angle 2$.

$$m\angle 1 + m\angle 2 + 40 = 180$$
$$m\angle 1 + m\angle 1 + 40 = 180$$
$$2m\angle 1 = 140$$
$$m\angle 1 = 70$$
$$m\angle 2 = 70$$

Finally, because $\angle 2$ and $\angle 3$ are complementary, $m\angle 3 = 20$.

Exercises

Find the measures of the numbered angles in each rectangle.

1.
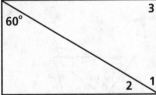

2.
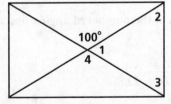

3.
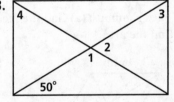

Find the measures of the numbered angles in each rhombus.

4.
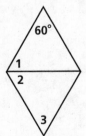

5.
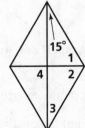

6.

Practice 6-4

For each parallelogram, (a) choose the best name, and then (b) find the
measures of the numbered angles.

1.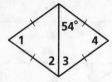

2.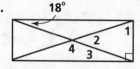

3.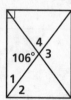

4.

5.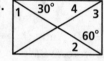

6.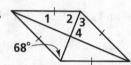

The parallelograms below are not drawn to scale. Can the parallelogram
have the conditions marked? If not, write *impossible.* Explain your answer.

7.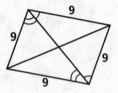

8.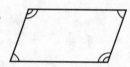

9.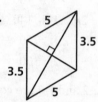

HIJK is a rectangle. Find the value of *x* and the length of each diagonal.

10. $HJ = x$ and $IK = 2x - 7$

11. $HJ = 3x + 5$ and $IK = 5x - 9$

12. $HJ = 3x + 7$ and $IK = 6x - 11$

13. $HJ = 19 + 2x$ and $IK = 3x + 22$

For each rhombus, (a) find the measures of the numbered angles, and then
(b) find the area.

14.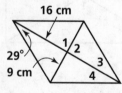

15. $AC = 8$ in.
$BD = 22$ in.

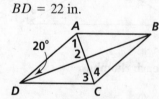

16.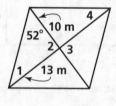

Determine whether the quadrilateral can be a parallelogram. If not, write
impossible. Explain your answer.

17. One pair of opposite sides is parallel, and the other pair is congruent.

18. Opposite angles are congruent and supplementary, but the quadrilateral
is not a rectangle.

Reteaching 6-5

Trapezoids and Kites

OBJECTIVE: Using triangle congruence and two-column proofs to find angle measures in trapezoids and kites	**MATERIALS:** None

Example

Write a two-column proof to identify three pairs of congruent triangles in kite *FGHJ*.

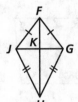

Statements	**Reasons**
1. $m\angle FKG = m\angle GKH = m\angle HKJ = m\angle JKF = 90$	1. Theorem 6-17
2. $\overline{FG} \cong \overline{FJ}$	2. Given
3. $\overline{FK} \cong \overline{FK}$	3. Reflexive Property of Congruence
4. $\triangle FKG \cong \triangle FKJ$	4. HL Theorem
5. $\overline{JK} \cong \overline{KG}$	5. CPCTC
6. $\overline{KH} \cong \overline{KH}$	6. Reflexive Property of Congruence
7. $\triangle JKH \cong \triangle GKH$	7. SAS Postulate
8. $\overline{JH} \cong \overline{GH}$	8. Given
9. $\overline{FH} \cong \overline{FH}$	9. Reflexive Property of Congruence
10. $\triangle FJH \cong \triangle FGH$	10. SSS Postulate

So $\triangle FKG \cong \triangle FKJ$, $\triangle JKH \cong \triangle GKH$, and $\triangle FJH \cong \triangle FGH$.

Exercises

In kite *FGHJ* in the example, $m\angle JFK = 38$ and $m\angle KGH = 63$. Find the following angle measures.

1. $m\angle FKJ$ 2. $m\angle FJK$ 3. $m\angle FKG$

4. $m\angle KFG$ 5. $m\angle FGK$ 6. $m\angle GKH$

7. $m\angle KHG$ 8. $m\angle KJH$ 9. $m\angle JHK$

10. Write a two-column proof to identify three pairs of congruent triangles in isosceles trapezoid *LMNP*.

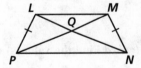

In isosceles trapezoid *LMNP*, $m\angle LPQ = 45$, $m\angle QMN = 87$, and $m\angle PQN$ is 12 less than 6 times $m\angle QNP$. Find the following angle measures.

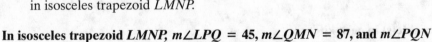

11. $m\angle PLQ$ 12. $m\angle LQP$ 13. $m\angle MNQ$

14. $m\angle MQN$ 15. $m\angle QNP$ 16. $m\angle QPN$

17. $m\angle PQN$ 18. $m\angle LMQ$ 19. $m\angle LQM$

20. Use isosceles trapezoid *LMNP* to explain why in Chapter 4 you did not learn about an Angle-Angle-Angle Theorem to prove triangles congruent.

Practice 6-5

Find the measures of the numbered angles in each isosceles trapezoid.

1.

2.

3.

4.

5.

6.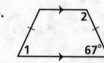

Algebra **Find the value(s) of the variable(s) in each isosceles trapezoid.**

7.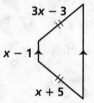

8.

9.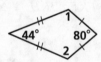

Find the measures of the numbered angles in each kite.

10.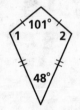

11.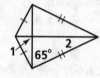

12.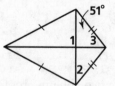

13.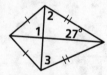

14.

15.

Algebra **Find the value(s) of the variable(s) in each kite.**

16.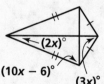

17.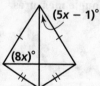

18.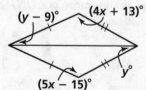

Name _____ Class _____ Date _____

Reteaching 6-6

Placing Figures in the Coordinate Plane

OBJECTIVE: Choosing convenient placement of figures on coordinate axes	**MATERIALS:** None

Example

Use the properties of each figure to find the missing coordinates.

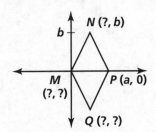

rhombus *MNPQ*

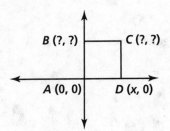

square *ABCD*

M is at the origin $(0, 0)$. Because diagonals of a rhombus bisect each other, *N* has *x*-coordinate $\frac{a}{2}$. Because the *x*-axis is a horizontal line of symmetry for the rhombus, *Q* has coordinates $(\frac{a}{2}, -b)$.

Because all sides are congruent, *B* has coordinates $(0, x)$. Because all angles are right, *C* has coordinates (x, x).

Exercises

Use the properties of each figure to find the missing coordinates.

1. parallelogram *OPQR*

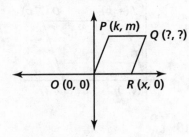

2. rhombus *XYZW*

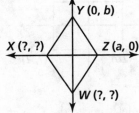

3. square *QRST*

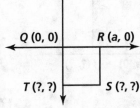

4. A quadrilateral has vertices at $(a, 0), (-a, 0), (0, a),$ and $(0, -a)$. Show that it is a square.

5. A quadrilateral has vertices at $(a, 0), (0, a + 1), (-a, 0)$ and $(0, -a - 1)$. Show that it is a rhombus.

6. Isosceles trapezoid *ABCD* has vertices $A(0, 0), B(x, 0),$ and $D(k, m)$. Find the coordinates of *C* in terms of *x*, *k*, and *m*. Assume $\overline{AB} \parallel \overline{CD}$.

Practice 6-6

Placing Figures in the Coordinate Plane

Find the coordinates of the midpoint of each segment and find the length
of each segment.

1. $\overline{ME}$

2. $\overline{ET}$

3. $\overline{TR}$

4. $\overline{RM}$

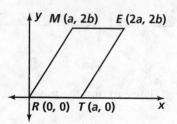

Find the slope of each segment.

5. $\overline{DI}$

6. $\overline{IR}$

7. $\overline{RE}$

8. $\overline{DE}$

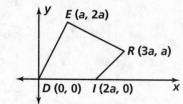

9. $\overline{VE}$

10. $\overline{ER}$

11. $\overline{RB}$

12. $\overline{VB}$

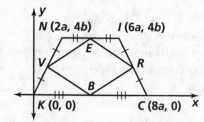

Use the properties of each figure to find the missing coordinates.

13. square

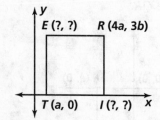

14. rectangle

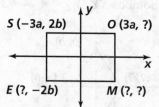

15. parallelogram

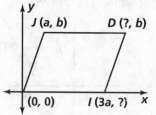

16. rhombus

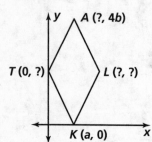

17. isosceles trapezoid

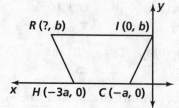

18. kite

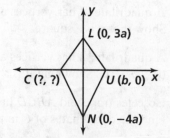

Name _____ Class _____ Date _____

Reteaching 6-7

Proofs Using Coordinate Geometry

OBJECTIVE: Proving theorems using figures in the coordinate plane	**MATERIALS:** None

Example

Use coordinate geometry to prove that the diagonals of a rectangle are congruent.

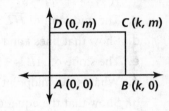

$AC = \sqrt{(k - 0)^2 + (m - 0)^2}$

$= \sqrt{k^2 + m^2}$

$BD = \sqrt{(0 - k)^2 + (m - 0)^2}$

$= \sqrt{(-k)^2 + m^2}$

$= \sqrt{k^2 + m^2}$

$\overline{AC} \cong \overline{BD}$

Exercises

Use coordinate geometry and the figures provided to prove the theorems.

1. Diagonals of an isosceles trapezoid are congruent.

2. The line containing the midpoints of two sides of a triangle is parallel to the third side.

3. The segments joining the midpoints of a rectangle form a rhombus.

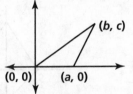

4. The segments joining the midpoints of a rhombus form a rectangle.

5. The median to the base of an isosceles triangle is perpendicular to the base.

6. The segments joining the midpoints of a quadrilateral form a parallelogram.

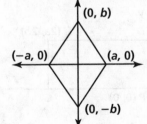

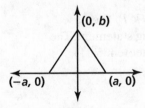

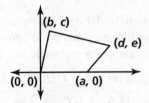

Geometry Chapter 6

Lesson 6-7 Reteaching

75

Practice 6-7

Proofs Using Coordinate Geometry

1. Given $\triangle HAL$ with perpendicular bisectors i, b, and m, complete the following to show that i, b, and m intersect in a point.

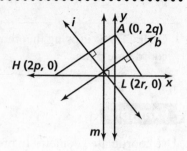

   a. The slope of $\overline{HA}$ is $\frac{-q}{p}$. What is the slope of line i?

   b. The midpoint of $\overline{HA}$ is (p, q). Show that the equation of line i is $y = \frac{p}{q}x + q - \frac{p^2}{q}$.

   c. The midpoint of $\overline{HL}$ is $(r + p, 0)$. What is the equation of line m?

   d. Show that lines i and m intersect at $(r + p, \frac{rp}{q} + q)$.

   e. The slope of $\overline{AL}$ is $\frac{-q}{r}$. What is the slope of line b?

   f. What is the midpoint of $\overline{AL}$?

   g. Show that the equation of line b is $y = \frac{r}{q}x + q - \frac{r^2}{q}$.

   h. Show that lines b and m intersect at $(r + p, \frac{rp}{q} + q)$.

   i. Give the coordinates for the point of intersection of i, b, and m.

Complete Exercises 2 and 3 without using any new variables.

2. *RHCP* is a rhombus.

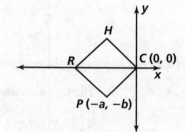

   a. Determine the coordinates of *R*.

   b. Determine the coordinates of *H*.

   c. Find the midpoint of $\overline{RH}$.

   d. Find the slope of $\overline{RH}$.

3. *ADFS* is a kite.

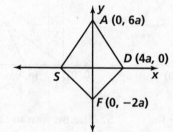

   a. Determine the coordinates of *S*.

   b. Find the midpoint of $\overline{AS}$.

   c. Find the slope of $\overline{AS}$.

   d. Find the midpoint of $\overline{DF}$.

   e. Find the slope of $\overline{DF}$.

4. Complete the coordinates for rectangle *DHCP*. Then use coordinate geometry to prove the following statement: The diagonals of a rectangle are congruent (Theorem 6-11).

   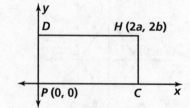

   Given: rectangle *DHCP*

   Prove: $\overline{DC} \cong \overline{HP}$

Reteaching 7-1

Areas of Parallelograms and Triangles

| **OBJECTIVE:** Finding areas of triangles and parallelograms | **MATERIALS:** Graph paper |

Example

A triangle has an area of 18 in.^{2} The length of its base is 6 in. Find its corresponding height.

Draw a sketch. Then substitute into the area formula, and solve for h.

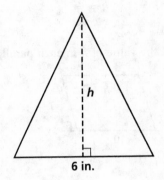

$A = \frac{1}{2}bh$

$18 = \frac{1}{2}(6)h$ Substitute.

$18 = 3h$ Simplify.

$h = 6$

The height of the triangle is 6 in.

Exercises

Complete each exercise.

1. Use graph paper. Draw an obtuse, an acute, and a right triangle, each with an area of 12 square units. Label the base and height of each triangle.

2. Draw a different obtuse, acute, and right triangle, each with an area of 12 square units. Label the base and height of each triangle.

3. A triangle has height 5 cm and base length 8 cm. Find its area.

4. A triangle has height 11 in. and base length 10 in. Find its area.

5. A triangle has area 24 m^2 and base length 8 m. Find its height.

6. A triangle has area 16 ft^2 and height 4 ft. Find its base.

7. A triangle has area 8 in.^{2} The lengths of the base and the height are equal. Find the length of its base.

8. On graph paper draw three parallelograms, each with an area of 24 square units. Label the base and height of each parallelogram.

9. A parallelogram has area 35 in.^{2} and height 7 in. Find its base.

10. A parallelogram has area 391 cm^2 and base 17 cm. Find its height.

11. A parallelogram has area 81 ft^2. The lengths of the base and the height are equal. Find the length of its base.

Name _____ Class _____ Date _____

Practice 7-1

Areas of Parallelograms and Triangles

Find the area of each triangle, given the base *b* and the height *h*.

1. $b = 4$, $h = 4$

2. $b = 8$, $h = 2$

3. $b = 20$, $h = 6$

4. $b = 40$, $h = 12$

5. $b = 3.1$, $h = 1.7$

6. $b = 4.8$, $h = 0.8$

7. $b = 3\frac{1}{4}$, $h = \frac{1}{2}$

8. $b = 8$, $h = 2\frac{1}{4}$

9. $b = 100$, $h = 30$

Find the value of *h* in each parallelogram.

10.

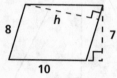

11.

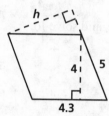

12.

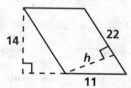

13. What is the area of $\square ABCD$ with vertices $A(-4, -6)$, $B(6, -6)$, $C(-1, 5)$, and $D(9, 5)$?

14. What is the area of $\triangle DEF$ with vertices $D(-1, -5)$, $E(4, -5)$, and $F(4, 7)$?

Find the area of the shaded region.

15.

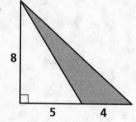

16.

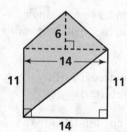

17.

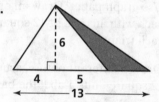

Find the area of each parallelogram.

18.

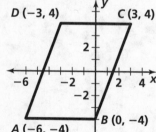

19.

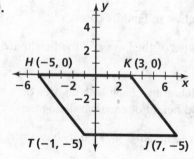

20.

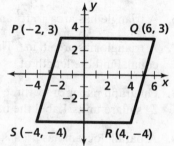

Reteaching 7-2

The Pythagorean Theorem and Its Converse

OBJECTIVE: Using the Pythagorean Theorem   **MATERIALS:** Graph paper

Example

Find the value of *g*. Leave your answer in simplest radical form.

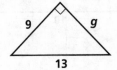

Using the Pythagorean Theorem, substitute *g* and 9 for the legs and 13 for the hypotenuse.

$a^2 + b^2 = c^2$

$g^2 + 9^2 = 13^2$ Substitute.

$g^2 + 81 = 169$ Simplify.

$g^2 = 88$ Subtract 81 from each side.

$g = \sqrt{88}$ Take the square root.

$g = \sqrt{4(22)}$ Simplify.

$g = 2\sqrt{22}$

Exercises

Complete each exercise.

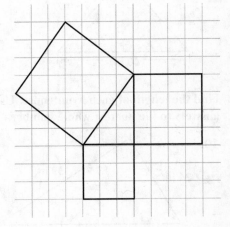

1. Draw a right triangle on graph paper so that the vertices are on the intersection of grid lines. Measure and label the lengths of the sides.

2. Construct a square on each side of the right triangle as shown.

3. Find the area of each square.

4. How does the sum of the areas of the two smaller squares compare with the area of the largest square?

5. What does this tell you about the relationship between the sides of the triangle?

Find the missing side lengths. Leave your answers in simplest radical form.

6.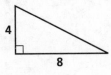

7.

8.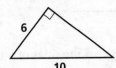

9.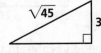

Practice 7-2

Pythagorean Theorem and Its Converse

Find the value of each variable. Leave your answers in simplest radical form.

1.
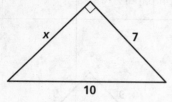

2.
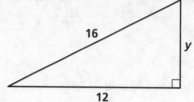

3.
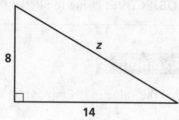

4.
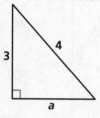

5.
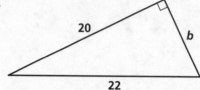

6.
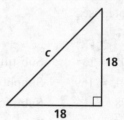

Find the area of each shaded region. Leave your answers in simplest radical form.

7.
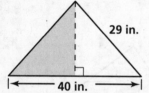

8.
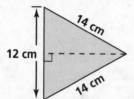

9.
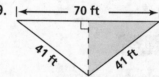

Find the length of each hypotenuse. Use your calculator, and round your answers to the nearest whole number.

10.
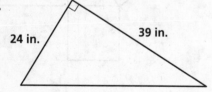

11.
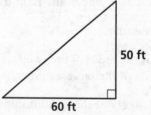

12.
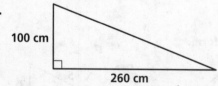

13.
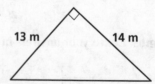

The numbers represent the lengths of the sides of a triangle. Classify each triangle as _acute_, _obtuse_, or _right_.

14. 6, 9, 10

15. 18, 24, 30

16. 20, 100, 110

17. 7, 24, 25

18. 2, 5, 6

19. 13, 21, 24

Reteaching 7-3

Special Right Triangles

• •

OBJECTIVE: Using the properties of a 30°-60°-90° triangle	**MATERIALS:** Centimeter grid paper, ruler, protractor

Example

Find the value of each variable.

$$5 = \sqrt{3}s$$ In a 30°-60°-90° triangle the length of the longer leg is $\sqrt{3}$ times the length of the shorter leg.

$$\frac{5}{\sqrt{3}} = s$$ Divide each side by $\sqrt{3}$.

$$s = \frac{5}{\sqrt{3}} \cdot \frac{\sqrt{3}}{\sqrt{3}} = \frac{5\sqrt{3}}{3}$$ Rationalize the denominator.

The length of the hypotenuse is twice the length of the shorter leg.

$$t = 2\left(\frac{5\sqrt{3}}{3}\right) = \frac{10\sqrt{3}}{3}$$

Exercises

Complete each exercise.

1. Draw a horizontal line segment on centimeter grid paper so that the endpoints are at the intersections of grid lines.

2. Use a protractor and a straightedge to construct a 30°-60°-90° triangle with your segment as one of its sides.

3. Use the 30°-60°-90° Triangle Theorem to calculate the lengths of the other two sides. Round to the nearest tenth.

4. Measure the lengths of the sides to the nearest tenth of a centimeter.

5. Compare your calculated results with your measured results.

6. Repeat the activity with a different segment.

For Exercises 7–10, find the value of each variable.

7.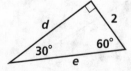

8.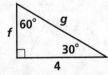

9.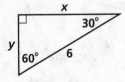

10.

• •

Practice 7-3

Find the value of each variable. Leave your answers in simplest radical form.

1.
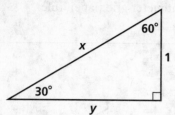

2.
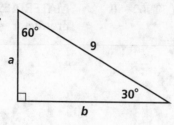

3.
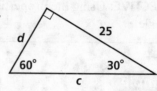

4.
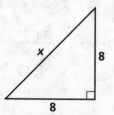

5.
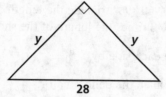

6.
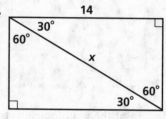

7.
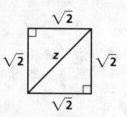

8.

9.

10. Find the length to the nearest centimeter of the diagonal of a square 30 cm on a side.

11. The hypotenuse of an isosceles right triangle is 8.4 in. Find the length of a side to the nearest tenth of an inch.

12. In a 30°-60°-90° triangle, the shorter leg is 6 ft long. Find the length to the nearest tenth of a foot of the other two sides.

13. Each side of a rhombus is 14 in. long. Two of the sides form a 60° angle. Find the area of the rhombus. Round your answer to the nearest square inch.

Algebra **Find the value of each variable. Leave your answers in simplest radical form.**

14.
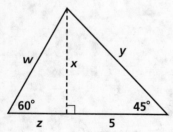

15.
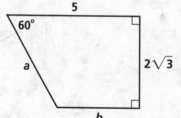

16.
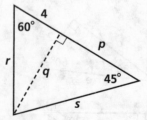

Reteaching 7-4

Areas of Trapezoids, Rhombuses, and Kites

OBJECTIVE: Finding areas of trapezoids and kites	**MATERIALS:** Centimeter grid paper

Example

Find the area of trapezoid *EFGH*.

You can draw two altitudes that divide the trapezoid into a rectangle and two congruent 45°-45°-90° triangles.

$\frac{24-16}{2} = \frac{8}{2} = 4$ Find the length of the base of each triangle.

Because the legs of a 45°-45°-90° triangle have the same length, $h = 4$.

$A = \frac{1}{2}h(b_1 + b_2)$ Use the formula for the area of a trapezoid.

$= \frac{1}{2} \cdot 4(16 + 24)$ Substitute.

$= 80$ Simplify.

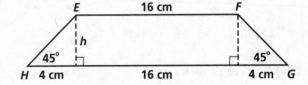

The area of trapezoid *EFGH* is 80 cm^2.

Exercises

Complete each exercise.

1. On centimeter grid paper, try to draw a trapezoid with area 48 cm^2.

2. Measure the bases and the height of the trapezoid.

3. Use the formula to calculate the actual area of the trapezoid.

4. Revise your figure until its area is 48 cm^2 or very close.

5. On centimeter grid paper, try to draw a kite with area 18 cm^2.

6. Measure the diagonals of the kite.

7. Use the formula to calculate the actual area of the kite.

8. Revise your figure until its area is 18 cm^2 or very close.

Find the area of each figure to the nearest tenth.

9.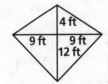

10.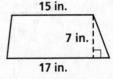

11.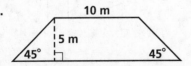

12.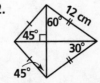

Name _____ Class _____ Date _____

Practice 7-4

Areas of Trapezoids, Rhombuses, and Kites

Find the area of each trapezoid.

1.
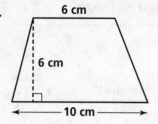

2.
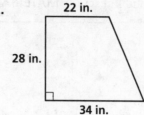

3.
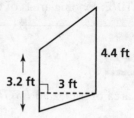

Find the area of each rhombus.

4.
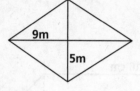

5.
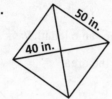

6.
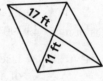

Find the area of each kite.

7.
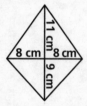

8.
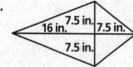

9.
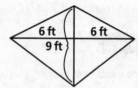

Find the area of each trapezoid. Leave your answers in simplest radical form.

10.
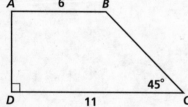

11.
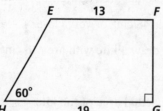

12.
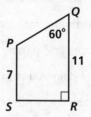

Find the area of each trapezoid to the nearest tenth.

13.
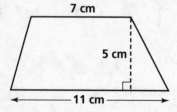

14.
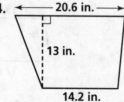

15.
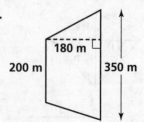

Reteaching 7-5

OBJECTIVE: Finding areas of regular polygons	**MATERIALS:** Graph paper

Example

Find the area of a regular quadrilateral (square) inscribed in a circle with radius 4 cm.

Draw one apothem to the base to form a 45°-45°-90° triangle. Using the 45°-45°-90° Triangle Theorem, find the length of the apothem.

$4 = \sqrt{2}a$ The hypotenuse $= \sqrt{2} \cdot$ leg in a 45°-45°-90° triangle.

$a = \dfrac{4}{\sqrt{2}}$ Simplify.

$a = \dfrac{4}{\sqrt{2}} \cdot \dfrac{\sqrt{2}}{\sqrt{2}} = 2\sqrt{2}$ Rationalize the denominator.

The apothem has the same length as the other leg, which is half as long as a side of the square. So the length of a side of the square is $2(2\sqrt{2})$ cm or $4\sqrt{2}$ cm. To find the square's area, use the formula for the area of a regular polygon.

$A = \dfrac{1}{2}ap$

$ = \dfrac{1}{2}(2\sqrt{2})(16\sqrt{2})$ $p = 4(4\sqrt{2}) = 16\sqrt{2}$

$ = 32$

The area of the regular quadrilateral is 32 cm^2.

Exercises

Complete each exercise.

1. Draw a square on graph paper.

2. Draw and label an apothem and a radius.

3. Measure the lengths of the apothem, the radius, and a side.

4. Check that the apothem equals half the length of a side.

5. Use a calculator to check that the apothem times $\sqrt{2}$ equals the radius.

Find the area of each square.

6.
5$\sqrt{2}$ in.

7.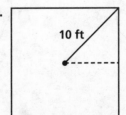
10 ft

8.
6 cm

9.
2 m

Practice 7-5

Areas of Regular Polygons

Find the values of the variables for each regular hexagon. Leave your answers in simplest radical form.

1.

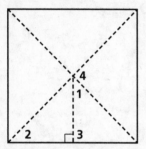

2.

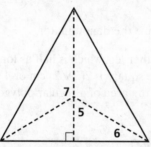

3.

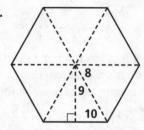

Each regular polygon has radii and an apothem as shown. Find the measure of each numbered angle.

4.

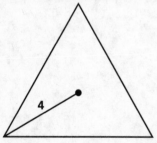

5.

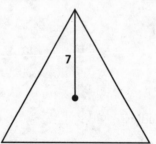

6.

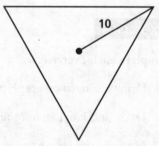

Find the area of each equilateral triangle, given the radius. Leave your answers in simplest radical form.

7.

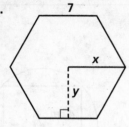

8.

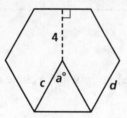

9.

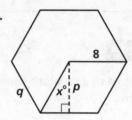

Find the area of each regular polygon to the nearest square inch.

10.

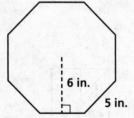

11.

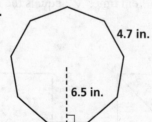

12.

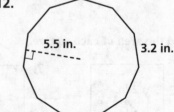

Reteaching 7-6

OBJECTIVE: Finding the length of an arc	**MATERIALS:** Compass, protractor, string, ruler

Example

Find the length of $\overset{\frown}{XY}$. Leave your answer in terms of π.

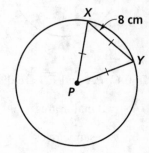

Because $\triangle XPY$ is an equilateral triangle and therefore equiangular, $m\angle XPY = 60$. This means that $m\overset{\frown}{XY} = 60$. Because $\overline{XY} \cong \overline{PY}$, the radius of $\odot P$ is 8.

$$\text{length of } \overset{\frown}{XY} = \frac{m\overset{\frown}{XY}}{360} \cdot 2\pi r \qquad \text{Use formula for arc length.}$$

$$= \frac{60}{360} \cdot 2\pi(8) \qquad \text{Substitute.}$$

$$= \frac{8\pi}{3} \qquad \text{Simplify.}$$

The length of $\overset{\frown}{XY}$ is $\frac{8\pi}{3}$ cm.

Exercises

Complete each exercise.

1. Draw a large circle with a central angle less than 180°.

2. Use a protractor to measure the central angle.

3. Use a ruler to measure the length of the radius.

4. Use the formula for arc length to find the length of the arc intercepted by the central angle.

5. Lay a piece of string along the circle. Mark the string at the endpoints of the arc. Measure the length of string between the marks using a ruler.

6. How does your calculated result compare with your measured result?

Find the length of each arc. Leave your answers in terms of π.

7. $\overset{\frown}{SV}$

8. $\overset{\frown}{UV}$

9. $\overset{\frown}{SUT}$

10. $\overset{\frown}{UTV}$

11. $\overset{\frown}{UT}$

12. $\overset{\frown}{VT}$

13. $\overset{\frown}{UVT}$

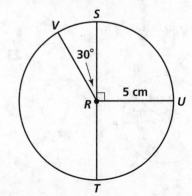

Practice 7-6

Circles and Arcs

Find the circumference of each circle. Leave your answers in terms of π.

1.
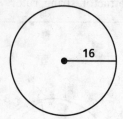

2.
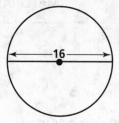

3.
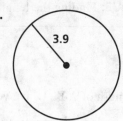

In ⊙C, $\overline{EA}$ and $\overline{FB}$ are diameters. Identify the following.

4. two major arcs

5. two minor arcs

6. two semicircles

7. a pair of adjacent arcs

8. an acute central angle

9. an obtuse central angle

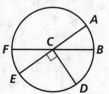

A market research survey found that adults' favorite vegetables are as shown below. Find the measure of the central angle for each of the following vegetables. Give your answers to the nearest degree.

10. potatoes

11. green beans

12. corn

13. carrots

14. broccoli

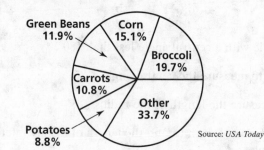

Source: *USA Today*

Find the measure of each arc in ⊙C.

15. $\overparen{AE}$

16. $\overparen{ED}$

17. $\overparen{DBA}$

18. $\overparen{AED}$

19. $\overparen{ABD}$

20. $\overparen{BD}$

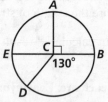

Find the length of each arc. Leave your answers in terms of π.

21. $\overparen{AB}$

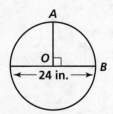

22. $\overparen{CDE}$

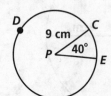

23. $\overparen{FH}$

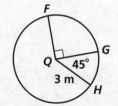

Reteaching 7-7

OBJECTIVE: Computing the areas of circles	**MATERIALS:** Graph paper

Example

Find the area of a circle with circumference 24π cm. Leave your answers in terms of π.

Use the formula for circumference, and solve for d.

$$C = \pi d$$
$$24\pi = \pi d$$
$$d = 24$$

Because the radius is half the diameter, $r = 12$ cm.

$$A = \pi r^2$$
$$= \pi \cdot 12^2$$
$$= 144\pi$$

The area of the circle is 144π cm^2.

Exercises

Complete each exercise.

1. On graph paper, draw a circle whose center is at the intersection of grid lines.

2. Find and label the length of a radius.

3. Estimate the area of the circle by counting the number of squares and parts of squares in the circle.

4. Calculate the area of the circle using the formula. Round your answer to the nearest tenth.

5. How does your calculated result compare with your estimated result?

6. Repeat the activity with a different size circle.

Compute the area of the circle. Leave your answers in terms of π.

7. circle with radius 5 ft

8. circle with radius 2 in.

9. circle with diameter 16 m

10. circle with diameter 9 ft

11. circle with circumference 36π cm

12. circle with circumference 16π in.

In $\odot Q$, sector PQR has an area of 27.2π cm^2 and $m\overset{\frown}{PR} = 50°$.

13. What is the length of the radius to the nearest centimeter?

14. What is the area of the circle to the nearest square centimeter?

Practice 7-7

The radius of ⊙*O* is 7. Find the area of each of the following. Leave your answers in terms of π.

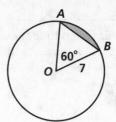

1. ⊙*O*

2. △*AOB*

3. sector *AOB*

4. the shaded segment

The radius of ⊙*P* is ½. Find the area of each of the following. Leave your answers in terms of π.

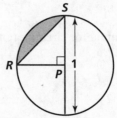

5. ⊙*P*

6. △*RPS*

7. sector *RPS*

8. the shaded segment

Find the area of each shaded sector of a circle. Leave your answers in terms of π.

9.

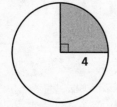

10.

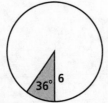

11.

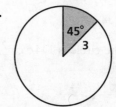

12.

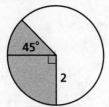

13.

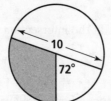

14.

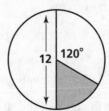

15.

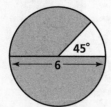

16.

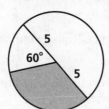

17.

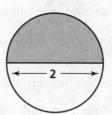

Find the area of each shaded segment of a circle. Round your answers to the nearest whole number.

18.

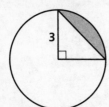

19.

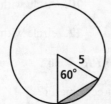

20.

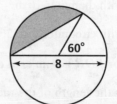

Geometry Chapter 7

Reteaching 7-8

OBJECTIVE: Using geometric models to find the probability of events	**MATERIALS:** Tacks, 3-in. by 5-in. index card, compass

Example

If a dart lands at random on the poster at the right, what is the probability that the dart will land inside one of the polygons?

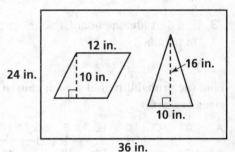

Find the sum of the areas of the polygons.

Area of polygons = Area of parallelogram + Area of triangle

$$= (12)(10) + \frac{1}{2}(10)(16)$$

$$= 120 + 80$$

$$= 200 \text{ in.}^2$$

Find the total area of the poster.

$$A = (24)(36) = 864 \text{ in.}^2$$

Calculate the probability.

$$P(\text{polygon}) = \frac{\text{area of polygons}}{\text{total area}}$$

$$= \frac{200}{864}$$

$$\approx 23\%$$

Exercises

Complete each exercise.

1. Use a compass to draw a circle with radius 1 in. on an index card.

2. Calculate the probability that if a tack is dropped on the card, its tip will land in the circle.

3. Lift a tack 12 in. above the index card and drop it. Repeat this 25 times. Record how many times the tip of the tack lands on the circle. (Ignore the times that the tack bounces off the card.) Calculate the experimental probability:

$$P = \frac{\text{number of times tip landed in circle}}{25}$$

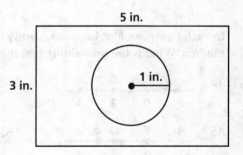

4. How do the probabilities you found in Exercises 2 and 3 compare?

5. If you repeated the experiment 100 times, what would you expect the results to be?

6. If a dart lands at random on the poster at the right, what is the probability that the dart will land in a circle?

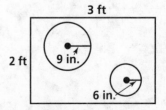

Practice 7-8

Geometric Probability

Use the dartboard at the right for Exercises 1–3.

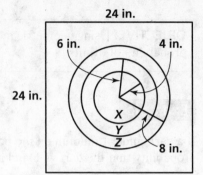

24 in.

6 in.   4 in.

24 in.

X
Y
Z

8 in.

1. If a dart hits the board, find the probability that it will land in region *X*.

2. If a dart hits the board, find the probability that it will land in region *Y*.

3. If a dart hits the board, find the probability that it will land in region *Z*.

Find the probability that a point chosen at random from $\overline{AK}$ is on the given segment.

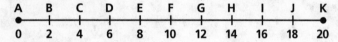

A	B	C	D	E	F	G	H	I	J	K
0	2	4	6	8	10	12	14	16	18	20

4. $\overline{CF}$ 5. $\overline{BI}$ 6. $\overline{GK}$

7. $\overline{FG}$ 8. $\overline{AK}$ 9. $\overline{AC}$

10. Roberto's trolley runs every 45 minutes. If he arrives at the trolley stop at a random time, what is the probability that he will *not* have to wait more than 10 minutes?

11. The state of Connecticut is approximated by a rectangle 100 mi by 50 mi. Hartford is approximately at the center of Connecticut. If a meteor hit the earth within 200 mi of Hartford, find the probability that the meteor landed in Connecticut.

12. A stop light at an intersection stays red for 60 seconds, changes to green for 45 seconds, and then turns yellow for 15 seconds. If Jamal arrives at the intersection at a random time, what is the probability that he will have to wait at a red light for more than 15 seconds?

In each figure, a point between *A* and *B* on the number line is chosen at random. What is the probability that the point is between *C* and *D*?

13.

	A	C	D		B
−2		0	2		4

14.

A	C		D		B
−10		0	10		20

15.

A		C		D	B
−2		0	2		4

16.

A		C		D	B
−3		0	3		6

Reteaching 8-1

OBJECTIVE: Using proportions to solve problems involving large numbers	**MATERIALS:** None

Example

About 15 of every 1000 lightbulbs assembled at the Brite Lite Company are defective. If the Brite Lite Company assembles approximately 13,000 lightbulbs each day, about how many are defective?

Set up a proportion to solve the problem. Let x represent the number of defective lightbulbs per day.

$$\frac{15}{1000} = \frac{x}{13,000}$$

$$15(13,000) = 1000x \qquad \text{Use the cross-product property.}$$

$$195,000 = 1000x$$

$$\frac{195,000}{1000} = x$$

$$195 = x$$

About 195 of the 13,000 lightbulbs assembled each day are defective.

Exercises

Use a proportion to solve each problem.

1. About 45 of every 300 apples picked at the Newbury Apple Orchard are rotted. If 3560 apples were picked one week, about how many apples were rotted?

2. A grocer orders 800 gallons of milk each week. He throws out about 64 gallons of spoiled milk each week. Of the 9600 gallons of milk he ordered over three months, about how many gallons of spoiled milk were thrown out?

3. Seven of every 20 employees at V & B Bank Company are between the ages of 20 and 30. If there are 13,220 employees at V & B Bank Company, how many are between the ages of 20 and 30?

4. About 56 of every 700 picture frames put together in an assembly line have broken pieces of glass. If 60,000 picture frames are assembled each month, about how many will have broken pieces of glass?

Algebra **Solve each proportion.**

5. $\dfrac{300}{1600} = \dfrac{x}{4800}$

6. $\dfrac{40}{140} = \dfrac{700}{x}$

7. $\dfrac{x}{2000} = \dfrac{17}{400}$

8. $\dfrac{35}{x} = \dfrac{150}{2400}$

9. $\dfrac{x}{1040} = \dfrac{290}{5200}$

10. $\dfrac{x}{42,000} = \dfrac{87}{500}$

11. $\dfrac{x}{380} = \dfrac{180}{5700}$

12. $\dfrac{1200}{90,000} = \dfrac{270}{x}$

13. $\dfrac{325}{x} = \dfrac{7306}{56,200}$

Practice 8-1

1. The Washington Monument in Washington, D.C., is about 556 ft tall. A three-dimensional puzzle of the Washington Monument is 24 in. tall. What is the ratio of the height of the puzzle to the height of the real monument?

Find the actual dimensions of each room.

2. playroom

3. library

4. master bedroom

5. bathroom

6. closet

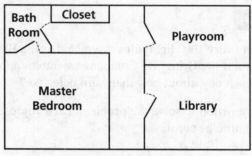

Scale: 1 in. = 16 ft

Algebra If $\frac{x}{y} = \frac{5}{8}$, which of the following must be true?

7. $8x = 5y$

8. $5x = 8y$

9. $\frac{y}{x} = \frac{8}{5}$

10. $\frac{x}{5} = \frac{y}{8}$

11. $\frac{x}{8} = \frac{y}{5}$

12. $\frac{x + y}{y} = \frac{13}{8}$

13. $\frac{x}{y} = \frac{10}{16}$

14. $\frac{x}{2y} = \frac{5}{4}$

15. $\frac{x}{x - y} = \frac{5}{3}$

Algebra Solve each proportion for *x*.

16. $\frac{x}{4} = \frac{9}{3}$

17. $\frac{6}{11} = \frac{x}{22}$

18. $\frac{6}{x} = \frac{2}{11}$

19. $\frac{7}{5} = \frac{x}{3}$

20. $\frac{2}{x} = \frac{x}{32}$

21. $\frac{3}{11} = \frac{8}{x}$

22. $\frac{x}{x + 2} = \frac{3}{4}$

23. $\frac{x + 1}{x} = \frac{7}{5}$

24. $\frac{5}{x} = \frac{3}{x + 1}$

For each rectangle, find the ratio of the longer side to the shorter side.

25.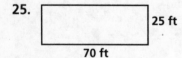
25 ft
70 ft

26.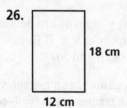
18 cm
12 cm

27.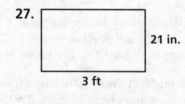
21 in.
3 ft

Complete each of the following.

28. If $3x = 8y$, then $\frac{x}{y} = \frac{?}{?}$.

29. If $\frac{a}{7} = \frac{b}{13}$, then $\frac{a}{b} = \frac{?}{?}$.

Reteaching 8-2

Similar Polygons

OBJECTIVE: Finding how to use ratio and proportion with similar polygons	**MATERIALS:** None

Example

Are the quadrilaterals similar? If they are, write a similarity statement, and give the similarity ratio. If they are not, explain.

Compare angles: $\angle A \cong \angle X$, $\angle B \cong \angle Y$, $\angle C \cong \angle Z$, $\angle D \cong \angle W$

Compare ratios of sides: $\dfrac{AB}{XY} = \dfrac{6}{3} = 2$ $\dfrac{CD}{ZW} = \dfrac{9}{4.5} = 2$

$\dfrac{BC}{YZ} = \dfrac{8}{4} = 2$ $\dfrac{DA}{WX} = \dfrac{4}{2} = 2$

Because corresponding sides are proportional and corresponding angles are congruent, $ABCD \sim XYZW$.

The similarity ratio of $ABCD$ to $XYZW$ is $2 : 1$.

Exercises

If the polygons are similar, write a similarity statement, and give the similarity ratio of the first figure to the second. If not, write *not similar*.

1.

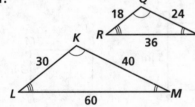

2.

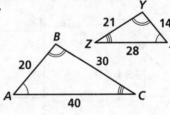

3.

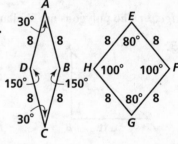

4.

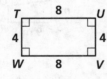

5.

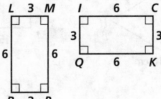

6.

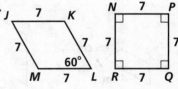

State whether the figures are similar. If so, give the similarity ratio.

7. a square with sides of length 10 and a square with sides of length 11

8. a rhombus with sides of length 4 containing a 30° angle and a rhombus with sides of length 4 containing a 40° angle

9. a rhombus with sides of length 4 containing a 50° angle and a rhombus with sides of length 9 containing a 130° angle

Practice 8-2

Are the polygons similar? If they are, write a similarity statement, and give
the similarity ratio. If they are not, explain.

1.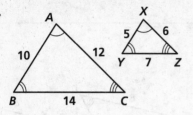

2.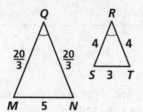

3.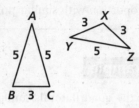

4.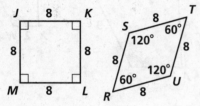

5.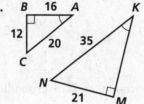

6.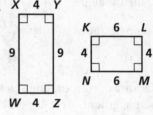

LMNO ~ HIJK. Complete the proportions and congruence statements.

7. $\angle M \cong$?   8. $\angle K \cong$?   9. $\angle N \cong$?

10. $\dfrac{MN}{IJ} = \dfrac{?}{JK}$ 11. $\dfrac{HK}{?} = \dfrac{HI}{LM}$ 12. $\dfrac{IJ}{MN} = \dfrac{HK}{?}$

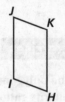

Algebra The polygons are similar. Find the values of the variables.

13.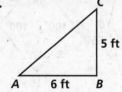

14.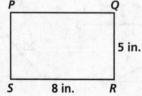

15.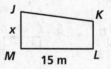

16.

$\triangle WXZ \sim \triangle DFG.$ Use the diagram to find the following.

17. the similarity ratio of $\triangle WXZ$ and $\triangle DFG$

18. $m\angle Z$ 19. DG 20. GF

21. $m\angle G$ 22. $m\angle D$ 23. WZ

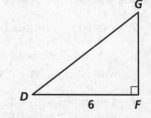

Reteaching 8-3

OBJECTIVE: Proving two triangles similar using the AA ~ Postulate and the SAS ~ and SSS ~ Theorems

MATERIALS: None

Example

Explain why the triangles are similar. Then write a similarity statement.

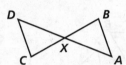

Given: $\overline{DC} \parallel \overline{BA}$

Because $\overline{DC} \parallel \overline{BA}$, $\angle A$ and $\angle D$ are alternate interior angles and are therefore $\cong$. The same is true for $\angle B$ and $\angle C$. So, by AA ~ Postulate, $\triangle ABX \sim \triangle DCX$.

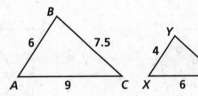

Compare the ratios of the lengths of sides:
$\frac{AB}{XY} = \frac{BC}{YZ} = \frac{CA}{ZX} = \frac{3}{2}$
So, by SSS ~ Theorem, $\triangle ABC \sim \triangle XYX$.

Exercises

Are the pairs of triangles similar? If so, state which postulate or theorem allows you to conclude this, and write a similarity statement. If not, write *not similar.*

1.

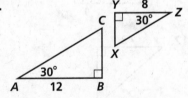

2.

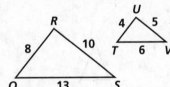

3.

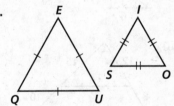

4.

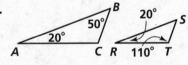

5.

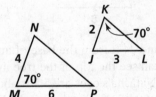

6.

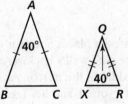

7. Are all equilateral triangles similar? Explain.

8. Are all isosceles triangles similar? Explain.

9. Are all congruent triangles similar? Are all similar triangles congruent? Explain.

Name _____ Class _____ Date _____

Practice 8-3

Explain why the triangles are similar. Write a similarity statement for each pair.

1.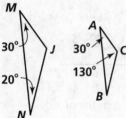

2.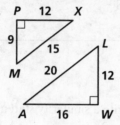

3.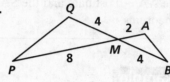

4.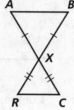

5.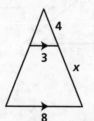

6.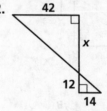

***Algebra* Find the value of x.**

7.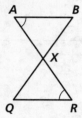

8.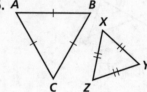

9.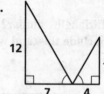

10.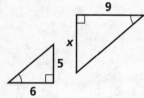

11.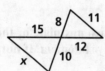

12.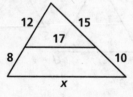

13. Natasha places a mirror on the ground 24 ft from the base of an oak tree. She walks backward until she can see the top of the tree in the middle of the mirror. At that point, Natasha's eyes are 5.5 ft above the ground, and her feet are 4 ft from the image in the mirror. Find the height of the oak tree.

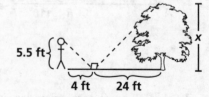

Geometry Chapter 8

Reteaching 8-4

Similarity in Right Triangles

> **OBJECTIVE:** Finding relationships between the lengths of the sides of a right triangle and the altitude to the hypotenuse
>
> **MATERIALS:** Calculator

Example

Solve for x, y, and z.

By the Pythagorean Theorem, $AB = 5$. Use the corollaries to Theorem 8-3 to find x, y, and z.

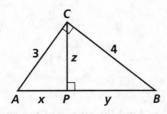

Corollary 2 gives you

$AB \cdot AP = (AC)^2$ $AB \cdot BP = (BC)^2$

$\quad\quad\quad 5x = 9 \quad\quad\quad\quad\quad\quad 5y = 16$

$\quad\quad\quad\;\; x = 1.8 \quad\quad\quad\quad\quad\quad y = 3.2$

Corollary 1 gives you

$\quad\quad (CP)^2 = AP \cdot BP$

$\quad\quad\quad z^2 = (1.8)(3.2)$

$\quad\quad\quad z^2 = 5.76$

$\quad\quad\quad\; z = 2.4$

Exercises

Find the values of the variables in each right triangle.

1.
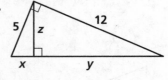

2.
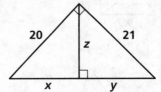

3.
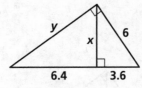

4.
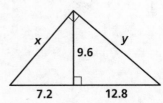

5.
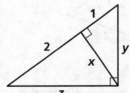

6.
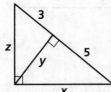

7. Find the length of the altitude to the hypotenuse of a right triangle whose sides have lengths 10, 24, and 26.

8. Find the length of the altitude to the hypotenuse of a right triangle whose legs have lengths 6 and 7.

9. Find a formula for the length of the altitude to the hypotenuse of a right triangle whose legs have lengths a and b.

Practice 8-4

Similarity in Right Triangles

Algebra **Find the geometric mean of each pair of numbers.**

1. 32 and 8
2. 4 and 16
3. 11 and 7

4. 2 and 22
5. 10 and 20
6. 6 and 30

Algebra **Refer to the figure to complete each proportion.**

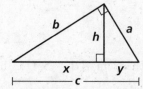

7. $\frac{x}{h} = \frac{?}{y}$
8. $\frac{a}{b} = \frac{?}{h}$
9. $\frac{a}{b} = \frac{h}{?}$

10. $\frac{a}{c} = \frac{y}{?}$
11. $\frac{a}{c} = \frac{h}{?}$
12. $\frac{b}{x} = \frac{?}{b}$

Algebra **Find the values of the variables.**

13.

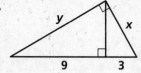

14.

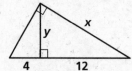

15.

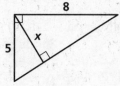

16.

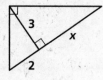

17.

18.

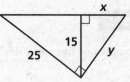

19.

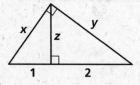

20.

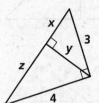

21.

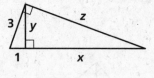

22. The altitude to the hypotenuse of a right triangle divides the hypotenuse into segments 6 in. and 10 in. long. Find the length *h* of the altitude.

Reteaching 8-5

OBJECTIVE: Investigating proportional relationships in triangles	**MATERIALS:** Calculator

Example

Find the value of each variable.

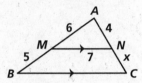

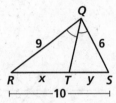

$\dfrac{AM}{MB} = \dfrac{AN}{NC}$ by the Side-Splitter Theorem

$\dfrac{6}{5} = \dfrac{4}{x}$ by substitution

$6x = 20$ by cross-multiplication

$x = \dfrac{10}{3}$

$\dfrac{QR}{QS} = \dfrac{RT}{ST}$ by the Triangle-Angle-Bisector Theorem

$\dfrac{9}{6} = \dfrac{x}{y}$ by substitution

$\dfrac{9}{6} = \dfrac{x}{10 - x}$ because $x + y = 10$

$9(10 - x) = 6x$ by cross-multiplication

$90 - 9x = 6x$

$90 = 15x$

$6 = x$

$4 = y$

Exercises

Find the value of each variable.

1.
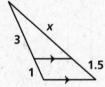

2.
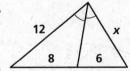

3.
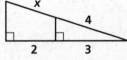

4.
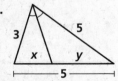

5.

6.
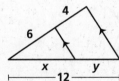

In $\triangle ABC$, $AB = 6$, $BC = 8$, and $AC = 9$.

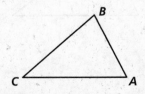

7. The bisector of $\angle A$ meets $\overline{BC}$ at point N. Find BN and CN.

8. $\overline{XY} \parallel \overline{CA}$. Point X lies on $\overline{BC}$ such that $BX = 2$, and Y is on $\overline{BA}$. Find BY.

Practice 8-5

Use the figure at the right to complete each proportion.

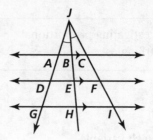

1. $\dfrac{AD}{DG} = \dfrac{?}{EH}$

2. $\dfrac{CF}{BE} = \dfrac{FI}{?}$

3. $\dfrac{JA}{JC} = \dfrac{AB}{?}$

4. $\dfrac{JF}{FE} = \dfrac{?}{DE}$

5. $\dfrac{GH}{HI} = \dfrac{?}{?}$

6. $\dfrac{AD}{AG} = \dfrac{?}{BH}$

Algebra **Find the values of the variables.**

7.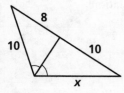

8.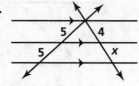

9.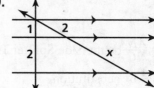

10.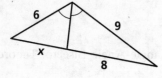

11.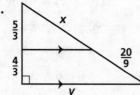

12.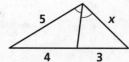

13.

14.

15.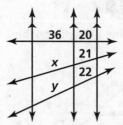

Algebra **Solve for x.**

16.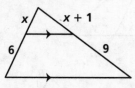

17.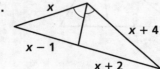

18.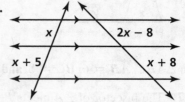

Reteaching 8-6

Perimeters and Areas of Similar Figures

OBJECTIVE: Finding the relationships between the similarity ratio and the perimeters and areas of similar figures	**MATERIALS:** None

Example

Each pair of figures is similar. Find the ratio of their perimeters and the ratio of their areas.

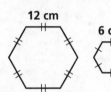

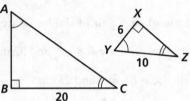

By Theorem 8-6, the ratio of the perimeters is $12 : 6 = 2 : 1$, and the ratio of the areas is $2^2 : 1^2 = 4 : 1$.

By AA ~ Postulate, $\triangle ABC \sim \triangle XYZ$ where $\overline{BC}$ and $\overline{XZ}$ are corresponding sides.
By the Pythagorean Theorem,
$$(XZ)^2 + (XY)^2 = (ZY)^2$$
$$(XZ)^2 + 6^2 = 10^2$$
$$(XZ)^2 = 64$$
$$XZ = 8$$
Therefore, by Theorem 8-6, the ratio of perimeters is $20 : 8 = 5 : 2$, and the ratio of areas is $5^2 : 2^2 = 25 : 4$.

Exercises

Each pair of figures is similar. Find the ratio of their perimeters and the ratio of their areas.

1.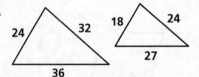

2.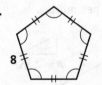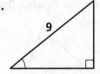

3.

$\triangle ACB$ is a right triangle with $BC = 3$, $AC = 4$, and $AB = 5$. $\overline{CN}$ is the altitude to the hypotenuse.

4. Find the ratio of the perimeter of $\triangle ANC$ to the perimeter of $\triangle CNB$.

5. Find the ratio of the perimeter of $\triangle ANC$ to the perimeter of $\triangle ACB$.

6. Find the ratio of the perimeter of $\triangle CNB$ to the perimeter of $\triangle ACB$.

7. Find the ratio of the area of $\triangle ANC$ to the area of $\triangle CNB$.

8. Find the ratio of the area of $\triangle ANC$ to the area of $\triangle ACB$.

9. Find the ratio of the area of $\triangle CNB$ to the area of $\triangle ACB$.

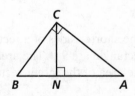

Practice 8-6

Perimeters and Areas of Similar Figures

For each pair of similar figures, find the ratio of the perimeters and the ratio of the areas.

1.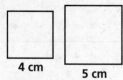
4 cm   5 cm

2.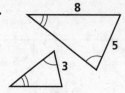
8   5   3

3.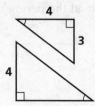
4   3   4

Find the similarity ratio of each pair of similar figures.

4. two regular hexagons with areas 8 in.^{2} and 32 in.^{2}

5. two squares with areas 81 cm^2 and 25 cm^2

6. two triangles with areas 10 ft^2 and 360 ft^2

7. two circles with areas 128π cm^2 and 18π cm^2

For each pair of similar figures, the area of the smaller figure is given. Find the area of the larger figure.

8.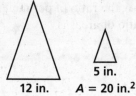
12 in.   5 in. $A = 20$ in.^{2}

9.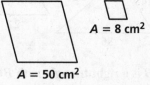
7 cm $A = 84$ cm^2 15 cm

10. 7 in.   5 in. $A = 18$ in.^{2} 8 in.

For each pair of similar figures, find the ratio of the perimeters.

11.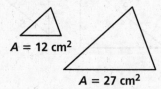
$A = 12$ cm^2 $A = 27$ cm^2

12.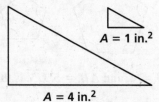
$A = 1$ in.^{2} $A = 4$ in.^{2}

13.
$A = 8$ cm^2 $A = 50$ cm^2

14. The shorter sides of a rectangle are 6 ft. The shorter sides of a similar rectangle are 9 ft. The area of the smaller rectangle is 48 ft^2. What is the area of the larger rectangle?

Reteaching 9-1

OBJECTIVE: Using tangents to determine side lengths in triangles

MATERIALS: Calculator

Example

Find the measure of the acute angle that the line $y - \frac{3}{4}x = 2$ makes with the x-axis. Round your answer to the nearest tenth.

The line $y - \frac{3}{4}x = 2$ can be rewritten $y = \frac{3}{4}x + 2$. Therefore, its slope is $\frac{3}{4}$.

$$\begin{aligned} \text{slope} &= \frac{\text{rise}}{\text{run}} \\ &= \frac{BO}{AO} \\ &= \tan A \end{aligned}$$

Therefore, $\tan A = \frac{3}{4}$.

Therefore, $m\angle BAO = \tan^{-1}\left(\frac{3}{4}\right) \approx 36.9$.

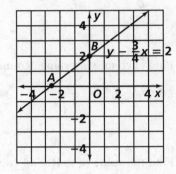

Exercises

Find the measure of the acute angle that the given line makes with the x-axis.

1. $y = \frac{1}{2}x - 2$

2. $y + 4x = 7$

3. $y = 6x + 10$

Find the measure of the acute angle that the given line makes with the y-axis.

4. $2x + y = 1$

5. $y = 7x$

6. $y = 70x$

In $\triangle ABC$, find the measures of $\angle A$ and $\angle B$ where $m\angle C = 90$.

7. $AC = 3, BC = 4, AB = 5$

8. $AC = 5, BC = 12, AB = 13$

9. $AC = 1, AB = 3$

10. $AC = 6, BC = 12$

11. The vertices of $\triangle JKL$ are $J(-2, 6)$, $K(-2, 0)$, and $L(-5, 0)$. Find the measure of $\angle J$.

12. Find the measure of $\angle L$ in Exercise 11.

13. Find the measure of the acute angle formed by the intersection of the lines $2y - x = 4$ and $y = 4x + 2$.

Practice 9-1

Write the tangent ratios for $\angle E$ and $\angle F$.

1.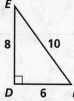

2.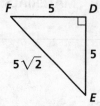

3.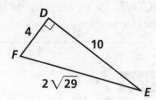

Find each missing value. Round your answers to the nearest tenth.

4. $\tan 46° = \dfrac{?}{12}$

5. $\tan \underline{\ ?\ } = \dfrac{3}{5}$

6. $\tan 12° = \dfrac{3}{?}$

Find the value of x. Round your answers to the nearest tenth.

7.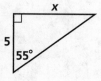

8.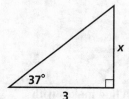

9.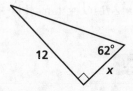

To the nearest tenth, find the measure of the acute angle that the given line forms with a horizontal line.

10. $y = 5x + 3$

11. $y = \dfrac{1}{2}x + 4$

12. $y = 3x - 6$

Find the value of x. Round your answers to the nearest degree.

13.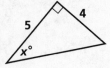

14.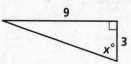

15.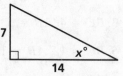

16.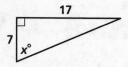

17.

18.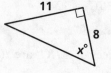

Reteaching 9-2

> **OBJECTIVE:** Using sine and cosine to determine unknown measures in right triangles
>
> **MATERIALS:** Calculator

Example

Find AC and BC to the nearest tenth.

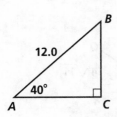

$\sin A = \dfrac{BC}{AB}$	Definition of sine
$\sin 40° = \dfrac{BC}{12.0}$	Substitute.
$BC = (\sin 40°)12.0$	Cross-multiply.
$BC = 7.7$	Use a calculator.
$\cos A = \dfrac{AC}{AB}$	Definition of cosine
$\cos 40° = \dfrac{AC}{12.0}$	Substitute.
$AC = (\cos 40°)12.0$	Cross-multiply.
$AC \approx 9.2$	Use a calculator.

Exercises

Find the missing lengths in each right triangle. Round your answers to the nearest tenth.

1.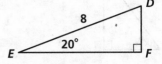

2.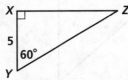

3.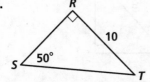

4. In $\triangle ABC$, $m\angle C = 90$, $m\angle A = 15$, and $AB = 6$. Find AC.

Find the measures of the acute angles of each right triangle. Round your answers to the nearest tenth of a degree.

5.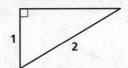

6.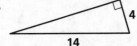

7.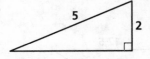

8. In $\triangle RST$, $\angle R$ is a right angle and $m\angle S = 32$. If the hypotenuse has length 4, find the lengths of the two legs.

9. A right triangle has a hypotenuse of length 10 and one leg of length 7.

    a. Find the length of the other leg using trigonometry.

    b. Find the length of the other leg using the Pythagorean Theorem.

Practice 9-2

Sine and Cosine Ratios

Write the ratios for sin *P* and cos *P*.

1.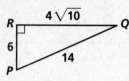

2.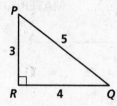

3.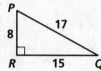

4.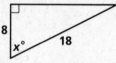

5.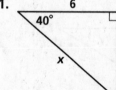

6.

Find the value of *x*. Round lengths of segments to the nearest tenth and angle measures to the nearest degree.

7.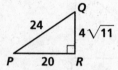

8.

9.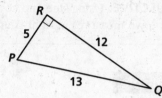

10.

11.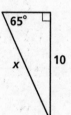

12.

13.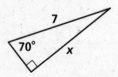

14.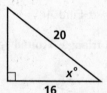

15.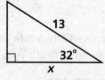

16.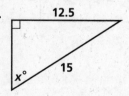

17.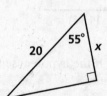

18.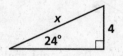

Reteaching 9-3

Angles of Elevation and Depression

OBJECTIVE: Using angles of elevation and depression and trigonometric ratios to solve problems

MATERIALS: Calculator

Example

A man standing 100 ft from a tall building measures the angle of elevation to the top of the building from the point where he is standing. If that angle is 62°, approximately how tall is the building?

In the diagram at the right,

$$\tan 62° = \frac{\text{height of building}}{100 \text{ ft}}$$

Cross-multiplying:

$$\text{height of building} = 100 \cdot (\tan 62°) \text{ ft}$$
$$= 188.07 \text{ ft}$$

The building is approximately 188 ft tall.

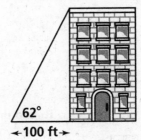

62°
←100 ft→

Exercises

Solve each problem. Drawing an accurate diagram will help.

1. You stand 40 ft from a tree. The angle of elevation from you to the top of the tree is 47°. How tall is the tree?

2. The angle of elevation to a building in the distance is 22°. You know that the building is approximately 450 ft tall. Estimate the distance to the base of the building.

3. An airplane is flying at an altitude of 10,000 ft. The airport at which it is scheduled to land is 50 mi away. Find the angle at which the airplane must descend for landing. (*Hint:* There are 5280 ft in 1 mi.)

4. A lake measures 600 ft across. A lodge stands on one shore. From your point on the opposite shore, the angle of elevation to the top of the lodge is 4°. How tall is the lodge?

5. A library wishes to build an access ramp for wheelchairs. The main entrance of the library is 8 ft above sidewalk level. If the architect recommends a grade (angle of elevation) of 6°, how long must the access ramp be?

6. Two buildings stand 90 ft apart at their closest points. At those points, the angle of depression from the taller building to the shorter building is 12°. How much taller is the taller building?

Practice 9-3

Angles of Elevation and Depression

Describe each angle as it relates to the diagram.

1. a. ∠1
   b. ∠2
   c. ∠3
   d. ∠4

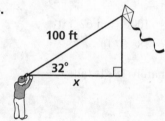

2. a. ∠1
   b. ∠2
   c. ∠3
   d. ∠4

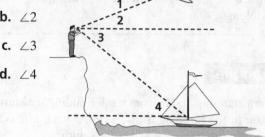

Find the value of *x*. Round the lengths to the nearest tenth.

3.

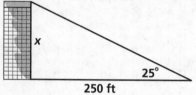

4.

5.

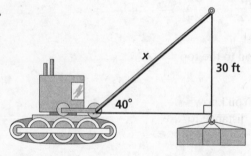

6.

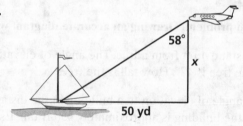

7.

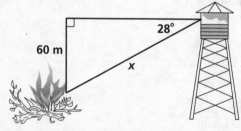

8.

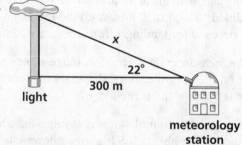

9. A person standing 30 ft from a flagpole can see the top of the pole at a 35° angle of elevation.

   a. Draw a diagram.

   b. The person's eye level is 5 ft from the ground. Find the height of the flagpole to the nearest foot.

Reteaching 9-4

> **OBJECTIVE:** Solving problems that involve vector addition
>
> **MATERIALS:** Calculator

Example

A boat heads directly across a river at 20 mi/h. The river is flowing downstream at 4 mi/h. Use vector addition to find the resultant path and speed of the boat.

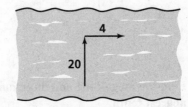

Because the boat heads directly across, its vector and the vector for the flow of the river are perpendicular. The vector that describes the resultant path of the boat is obtained using the head-to-tail method and the Pythagorean Theorem. That vector has length c where

$$c^2 = 20^2 + 4^2$$
$$c^2 = 416$$
$$c \approx 20.4$$

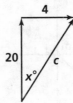

So the resultant speed is approximately 20.4 mi/h. In the diagram, the path is $x°$ east of north. Using trigonometry,

$$\tan x = \frac{4}{20} = 0.20$$
$$x \approx 11.3°$$

Exercises

Solve each problem. Drawing an accurate diagram will help.

1. A boat heads directly across a river at 8 mi/h. The river flows downstream at 10 mi/h. Find the resulting speed and direction of the boat. Round your answers to the nearest tenth.

2. A woman walks 6 mi due east from her home. She then walks 8 mi due south.
   a. How far is she from her home?
   b. In what direction should she walk to return home?

3. A bird heading directly south at 5 mi/h encounters a wind blowing due east at 3 mi/h. How would the direction of the bird be affected?

4. A boat heads directly across a river at 12 mi/h. The river is 3 mi wide. Upon disembarking, the boat's captain finds that the boat is 1 mi downstream from where he had intended to land. Find the speed of the river's current.

Practice 9-4

Describe each vector as an ordered pair. Give the coordinates to the nearest tenth.

1.

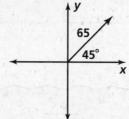

2.

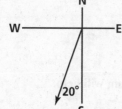

3.

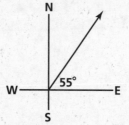

Find the magnitude and direction of each vector. Round your answers to the nearest tenth.

4.

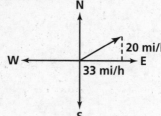

5.

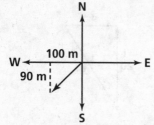

6.

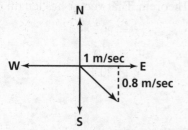

Use compass directions to describe the direction of each vector.

7.

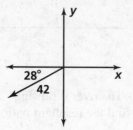

8.

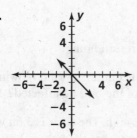

9.

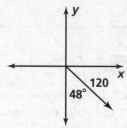

For Exercises 10–12, (a) write the resultant as an ordered pair, and (b) draw the resultant.

10.

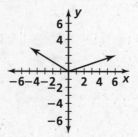

11.

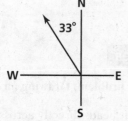

12.

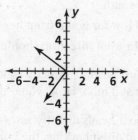

13. Sketch a vector that has the direction 48° south of east.

14. Sketch a vector that has the direction 30° west of north.

Reteaching 9-5

Trigonometry and Area

OBJECTIVE: Using trigonometry to find the areas of regular polygons	**MATERIALS:** Calculator

Example

Find the area of a regular hexagon with side 12 cm.

Area $= \frac{1}{2}ap$, where $a =$ apothem

$\qquad\qquad\qquad p =$ perimeter

$p = 6 \cdot 12 = 72$, because the figure is 6-sided.

Area $= \frac{1}{2}a(72) = 36a$

To find a, examine $\triangle AOB$ above. The apothem is measured along $\overline{OM}$, which divides $\triangle AOB$ into congruent triangles.

$$AM = \frac{1}{2}AB = 6$$

$$m\angle AOM = \frac{1}{2}m\angle AOB$$

$$= \frac{1}{2}\left(\frac{360}{6}\right)$$

$$= 30$$

Divide 360 by 6 because there are six congruent central angles.

So, by trigonometry, $\tan 30° = \dfrac{AM}{a}$

$$\tan 30° = \frac{6}{a}$$

$$a = \frac{6}{\tan 30°}$$

Finally, area $= \frac{1}{2}ap = \frac{1}{2}\left(\dfrac{6}{\tan 30°}\right)(72) \approx 374.1 \text{ cm}^2$.

Exercises

Find the area of each regular polygon.

1. Find the area of a regular octagon with side 2 in.

2. Find the area of a regular decagon with side 4 cm.

3. Find the area of a regular hexagon with apothem 5 in.

4. Find the area of a regular pentagon with side 10 in.

5. Find the area of a regular pentagon with apothem 10 in.

6. Find the area of a regular 20-gon with perimeter 40 in.

7. **a.** Find the area of a regular quadrilateral with side 9 in.

   b. What other method can be used to find the area?

Practice 9-5

Trigonometry and Area

Find the area of each polygon. Round your answers to the nearest tenth.

1. an equilateral triangle with apothem 5.8 cm

2. a square with radius 17 ft

3. a regular hexagon with apothem 19 mm

4. a regular pentagon with radius 9 m

5. a regular octagon with radius 20 in.

6. a regular hexagon with apothem 11 cm

7. a regular decagon with apothem 10 in.

8. a square with radius 9 cm

Find the area of each triangle. Round your answers to the nearest tenth.

9.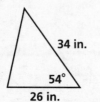
6.5 m 63° 13 m

10.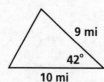
9 mi 42° 10 mi

11.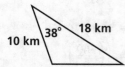
10 km 38° 18 km

12.
34 in. 54° 26 in.

13. 6 mm 46° 4.5 mm

14. 28 in. 59° 32 in.

15.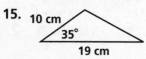
10 cm 35° 19 cm

16.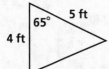
65° 5 ft 4 ft

17.
15 m 46° 15 m

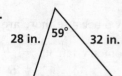

Find the area of each regular polygon to the nearest tenth.

18. a triangular dog pen with apothem 4 m

19. a hexagonal swimming pool cover with radius 5 ft

20. an octagonal floor of a gazebo with apothem 6 ft

21. a square deck with radius 2 m

22. a hexagonal patio with apothem 4 ft

Reteaching 10-1

OBJECTIVE: Drawing nets of various space figures	**MATERIALS:** Graph paper, scissors, tape

Example

Draw a net for the doorstop at the right.
Label the net with its appropriate dimensions.

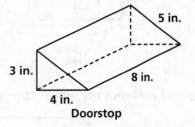

Doorstop

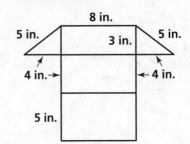

Exercises

Complete the following to verify Euler's Formula.

1. On graph paper, draw three other nets for the polyhedron shown above. Let each unit of length represent $\frac{1}{4}$ in.

2. Cut out each net, and use tape to form the solid figure.

3. Count the number of vertices, faces, and edges of one of the figures.

4. Verify that Euler's Formula, $F + V = E + 2$, is true for this polyhedron.

Draw a net for each three-dimensional figure.

5.
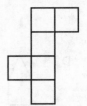

6.
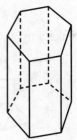

7.
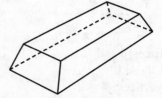

8.
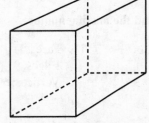

Practice 10-1

1. Choose the nets that will fold to make a cube.

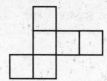   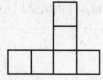   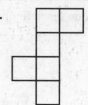   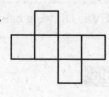

A.   B.   C.   D.

Draw a net for each figure. Label each net with its appropriate dimensions.

2.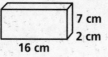
7 cm
2 cm
16 cm

3.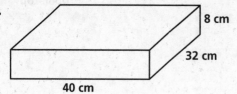
8 cm
32 cm
40 cm

4.
1 cm
2 cm
1 cm

Match each three-dimensional figure with its net.

5.   **6.**   **7.**   **8.**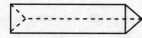

A. 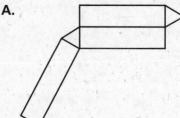   **B.** 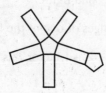   **C.**   **D.**

9. Choose the nets that will fold to make a pyramid with a square base.

A.   **B.**   **C.**   **D.**

Use Euler's Formula to find the missing number.

10. Faces: 5
Edges: ■
Vertices: 5

11. Faces: ■
Edges: 9
Vertices: 6

12. Faces: 8
Edges: 18
Vertices: ■

Reteaching 10-2

OBJECTIVE: Creating isometric and orthographic drawings

MATERIALS: Isometric dot paper

Example

Create an isometric drawing and an orthographic drawing of the cube structure at the right.

Isometric drawing:

First, draw the front edges of the figure.

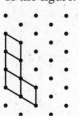

Next, draw the segments for the back edges of the figure.

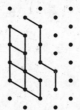

Complete by drawing the six segments joining the front and back edges.

Orthographic drawing:

From the front view, four squares are visible.

From the top view, two squares are visible.

From the right view, three squares are visible.

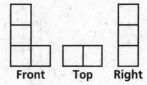

Exercises

Create (a) an isometric drawing and (b) an orthographic drawing of each cube structure.

1.   **2.**   **3.**   **4.**

5. Use the isometric drawing to create an orthographic drawing.

6. Use the orthographic drawing to create an isometric drawing.

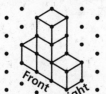

Name _____ Class _____ Date _____

Practice 10-2

Space Figures and Drawings

• •

Make an isometric drawing of each cube structure.

1.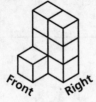

2.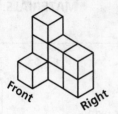

3.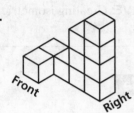

For each figure, (a) make a foundation drawing, and (b) make an orthographic drawing.

4.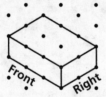

5.

6.

7.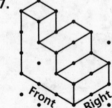

8.

9.

Describe the cross section in each diagram.

10.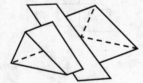

11.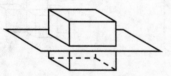

12.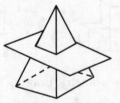

Draw and describe a cross section formed by a rectangular prism and the plane described.

13. a horizontal plane intersecting opposite faces of the prism

14. a vertical plane intersecting the front and right faces of the prism

Reteaching 10-3

OBJECTIVE: Finding lateral areas and surface areas of cylinders and prisms	**MATERIALS:** Centimeter grid paper, scissors, tape

Example

Draw a net for the cylinder to calculate its surface area.

From the net, we can see that the lateral surface area is a rectangle with length equal to the circumference of the base of the cylinder.

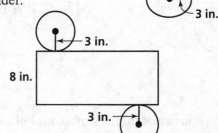

$$\begin{aligned} \text{Area of rectangle} &= b \cdot h \\ &= 2\pi r \cdot h \\ &= 2\pi(3) \cdot 8 \\ &= 48\pi \end{aligned}$$

Each base is a circle with radius 3 in.

$$\begin{aligned} \text{Area of base} &= \pi r^2 \\ &= \pi(3)^2 \\ &= 9\pi \end{aligned}$$

The surface area is the sum of the lateral area and the area of the two bases.

$$\begin{aligned} \text{S.A.} &= \text{L.A.} + 2B \\ &= 48\pi + 2(9\pi) \\ &= 66\pi \approx 207.3 \end{aligned}$$

The surface area of the cylinder is about 207.3 in.^{2}

Exercises

Use the net at the right to complete the following.

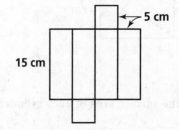

1. Draw the net at the right on centimeter grid paper.

2. Cut out the net, and tape it together to make a prism.

3. Find the lateral area and surface area of the prism.

Find the surface area of each figure. Round your answers to the nearest tenth, if necessary.

4.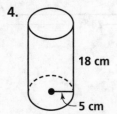

5.

6.

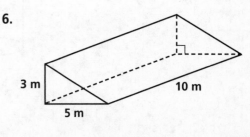

Practice 10-3

Surface Areas of Prisms and Cylinders

Find the lateral area of each cylinder to the nearest tenth.

1.
2 cm
$d = 10$ cm

2.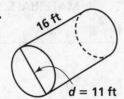
16 ft
$d = 11$ ft

3.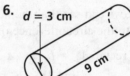
$d = 9$ cm
8 cm

4.
$r = 3$ m
6 m

5.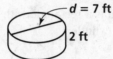
$d = 7$ ft
2 ft

6.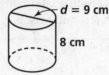
$d = 3$ cm
9 cm

Find (a) the lateral area and (b) the surface area of each prism. Round your answers to the nearest whole number.

7.
8 m   15 m
8 m

8.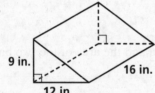
9 in.   16 in.
12 in.

9.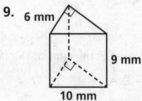
6 mm
9 mm
10 mm

10.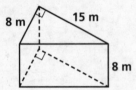
4 cm   3 cm
4 cm

11.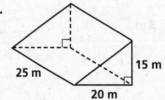
25 m   15 m
20 m

12.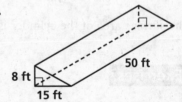
50 ft
8 ft
15 ft

Find the surface area of each cylinder in terms of π.

13.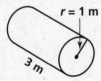
$r = 1$ m
3 m

14.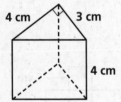
$d = 7$ cm
10 cm

15.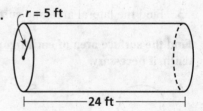
$r = 5$ ft
24 ft

Reteaching 10-4

OBJECTIVE: Finding lateral areas and surface areas of cones and pyramids

MATERIALS: Graph paper, scissors, tape

Example

Find the surface area of a cone with slant height 18 cm and height 12 cm.

Begin by drawing a sketch.

Use the Pythagorean Theorem to find r, the radius of the base of the cone.

$$r^2 + 12^2 = 18^2$$
$$r^2 + 144 = 324$$
$$r^2 = 180$$
$$r \approx 13.4$$

Now substitute into the formula for the surface area of a cone.

$$\begin{aligned}
S.A. &= L.A. + B \\
&= \pi r l + \pi r^2 \\
&= \pi(13.4)(18) + \pi(13.4)^2 \\
&\approx 1321.9
\end{aligned}$$

The surface area of the cone is about 1321.9 cm^2.

Exercises

Use graph paper, scissors, and tape to complete the following.

1. Draw a net of a square pyramid on graph paper.

2. Cut it out, and tape it together.

3. Measure its base length and slant height.

4. Find the surface area of the pyramid.

In Exercises 5–8, round your answers to the nearest tenth, if necessary.

5. Find the surface area of a square pyramid with base length 16 cm and slant height 20 cm.

6. Find the surface area of a cone with radius 5 m and slant height 15 m.

7. Find the surface area of a square pyramid with base length 10 in. and height 15 in.

8. Find the surface area of a cone with radius 6 ft and height 11 ft.

Practice 10-4

Find the lateral area of each cone to the nearest whole number.

1.
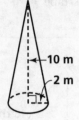
←10 m
2 m

2.
←20 cm
9 cm

3.
8 ft
6 ft

Find the surface area of each cone in terms of π.

4.
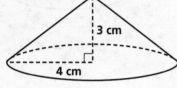
3 cm
4 cm

5.
16 m
30 m

6.
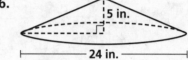
5 in.
24 in.

Find the lateral area of each regular pyramid to the nearest tenth.

7.
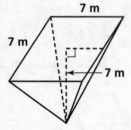
7 m
7 m
7 m

8.
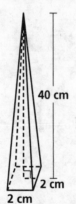
40 cm
2 cm
2 cm

9.
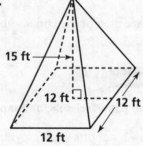
15 ft
12 ft
12 ft
12 ft

Find the surface area of each regular pyramid to the nearest tenth.

10.
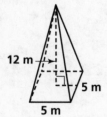
12 m
5 m
5 m

11.
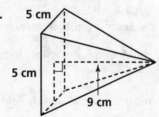
5 cm
5 cm
9 cm

12.
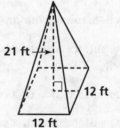
21 ft
12 ft
12 ft

Reteaching 10-5

OBJECTIVE: Finding the volumes of cylinders and prisms

MATERIALS: None

Example

Which is greater: the volume of the cylinder or the volume of the prism?

Volume of the cylinder: $V = Bh$
$$= \pi r^2 \cdot h$$
$$= \pi (3)^2 \cdot 12$$
$$\approx 339.3$$

Volume of prism: $V = Bh$
$$= s^2 \cdot h$$
$$= 6^2 \cdot 12$$
$$= 432$$

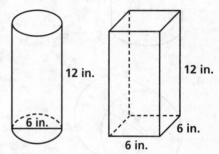

The volume of the cylinder is about 339.3 in.^{3} The volume of the prism is 432 in.^{3} The volume of the prism is greater.

Exercises

Find the volume of each object.

1. the rectangular prism part of the milk container

2. the cylinder part of the measuring cup

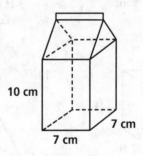

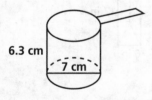

Find the volume of each of the following. Round your answers to the nearest tenth, if necessary.

3. a square prism with base length 7 m and height 15 m

4. a cylinder with radius 9 in. and height 10 in.

5. a triangular prism with height 14 ft and a right triangle base with legs measuring 9 ft and 12 ft

6. a cylinder with diameter 24 cm and height 5 cm

Practice 10-5

Find the volume of each cylinder to the nearest tenth.

1.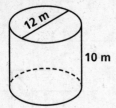
12 m
10 m

2.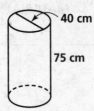
40 cm
75 cm

3.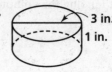
3 in.
1 in.

4.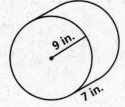
9 in.
7 in.

5.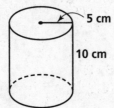
5 cm
10 cm

6.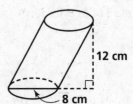
12 cm
8 cm

Find the volume of each prism to the nearest whole number.

7.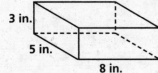
3 in.
5 in.
8 in.

8.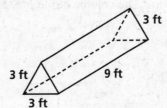
3 ft
3 ft
9 ft
3 ft

9.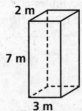
2 m
7 m
3 m

10.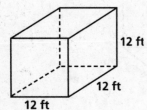
12 ft
12 ft
12 ft

11.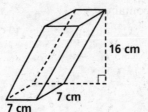
16 cm
7 cm
7 cm

12.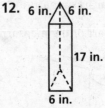
6 in.   6 in.
17 in.
6 in.

Find the volume of each composite figure to the nearest whole number.

13.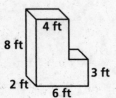
4 ft
8 ft
3 ft
2 ft
6 ft

14.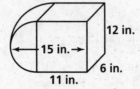
12 in.
15 in.
6 in.
11 in.

15.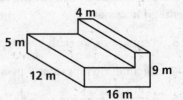
4 m
5 m
9 m
12 m
16 m

Reteaching 10-6

| **OBJECTIVE:** Finding volumes of cones and pyramids | **MATERIALS:** None |

Example

Calculate the volume of the cone.

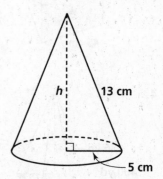

Find the height of the cone.

$13^2 = h^2 + 5^2$	Use the Pythagorean Theorem.
$169 = h^2 + 25$	Substitute.
$h^2 = 144$	Simplify.
$h = 12$	Take the square root of each side.

Find the volume of the cone.

$V = \frac{1}{3}\pi r^2 h$	Use the formula for the volume of a cone.
$= \frac{1}{3}\pi(5)^2 \cdot 12$	Substitute.
$= 100\pi$	Simplify.
≈ 314.2	

The volume of the cone is about 314.2 cm^2.

Exercises

1. From the figures shown below, choose the pyramid with volume closest to the volume of the cone at the right.

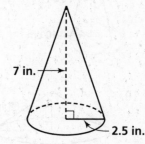

A.

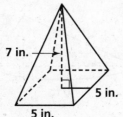

B.

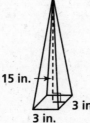

C.

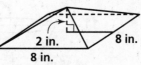

Find the volume of each figure. Round your answers to the nearest tenth, if necessary.

2.

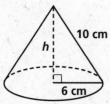

3.

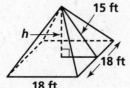

4.

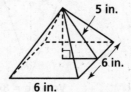

5.

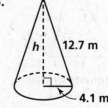

Practice 10-6

Find the volume of each pyramid.

1.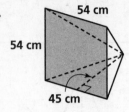
54 cm
54 cm
45 cm

2.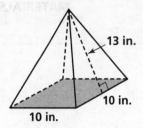
13 in.
10 in.
10 in.

3.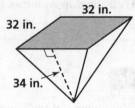
32 in.
32 in.
34 in.

4.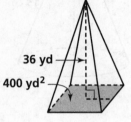
36 yd
400 yd²

5.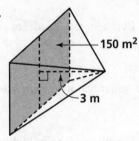
150 m²
3 m

6.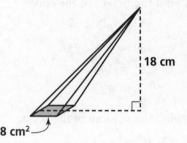
18 cm
8 cm²

Find the volume of each cone. Round your answers to the nearest tenth.

7.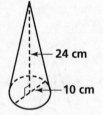
24 cm
10 cm

8.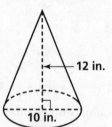
12 in.
10 in.

9.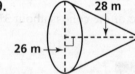
28 m
26 m

10.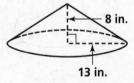
8 in.
13 in.

11.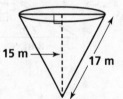
15 m
17 m

12.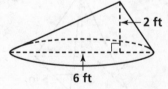
2 ft
6 ft

Algebra **Find the value of the variable in each figure.**

13.
x
15
15
Volume = 1500

14.
x
6
Volume = 8π

15.
14
9   x
Volume = 126

Reteaching 10-7

OBJECTIVE: Calculating the surface areas and volumes of spheres

MATERIALS: Compass, scissors, tape

Example

Find the surface area and volume of the sphere.

Substitute $r = 5$ into each formula, and simplify.

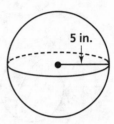

$$S.A. = 4\pi r^2 \qquad\qquad V = \tfrac{4}{3}\pi r^3$$
$$= 4\pi(5)^2 \qquad\qquad = \tfrac{4}{3}\pi(5)^3$$
$$= 100 \qquad\qquad = \tfrac{500\pi}{3}$$
$$\approx 314.2 \qquad\qquad \approx 523.6$$

The surface area of the sphere is about 314.2 in.^{2} The volume of the sphere is about 523.6 in.^{3}

Exercises

Use the figures at the right to guide you in completing the following.

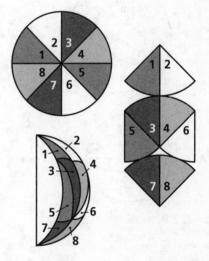

1. Use a compass to draw two circles, each with radius 3 in. Cut out each circle.

2. Fold one circle in half three successive times. Number the central angles 1 through 8.

3. Cut out the sectors, and tape them together as shown.

4. Take the other circle, fold it in half, and tape it to the rearranged circle so that they form a quadrant of a sphere.

5. The area of one circle has covered one quadrant of a sphere. How many circles would cover the entire sphere?

6. How is the radius of the sphere related to the radius of the circle?

Find the volume and surface area of a sphere with the given radius or diameter. Round your answers to the nearest tenth, if necessary.

7. $r = 3$ in.

8. $d = 10$ cm

9. $r = 12$ m

10. $d = 25$ ft

11. $r = 6.3$ in.

12. $d = 8.4$ mm

Practice 10-7

Find the surface area of each sphere. Round your answers to the nearest tenth.

1.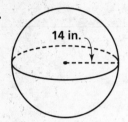
14 in.

2.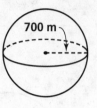
700 m

3.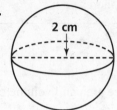
2 cm

4.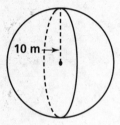
10 m

5.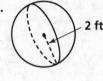
2 ft

6.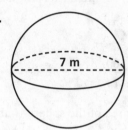
7 m

Find the volume of each sphere. Round your answers to the nearest tenth.

7.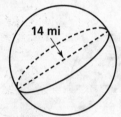
14 mi

8.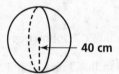
40 cm

9.
12 m

10.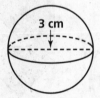
3 cm

11.
S.A. = 90,790 cm²

12.
S.A. = 45,240 yd²

The volume of each sphere is given. Find the surface area. Round your answers to the nearest whole number.

13. $V = 1200 \text{ ft}^3$

14. $V = 750 \text{ m}^3$

15. $V = 4500 \text{ cm}^3$

Use the given circumference to approximate the volume of each object. Round your answers to the nearest whole number.

16. a baseball with $C = 24$ cm

17. a basketball with $C = 75$ cm

18. a volleyball with $C = 69$ cm

19. a golf ball with $C = 13.5$ cm

Reteaching 10-8

OBJECTIVE: Finding the relationships between the similarity ratio and the ratios of the areas and volumes of similar solids	**MATERIALS:** Calculator

Example

The pyramids shown are similar, and they have volumes of 216 in.^{3} and 125 in.^{3} The larger pyramid has surface area 250 in.^{2}

Find the ratio of their surface areas, and find the surface area of the smaller pyramid.

By Theorem 10-12, if similar solids have similarity ratio $a : b$, then the ratio of their volumes is $a^3 : b^3$. So

$$\frac{a^3}{b^3} = \frac{216}{125}$$

$$\frac{a}{b} = \frac{6}{5} \qquad \text{Take the cube root of both sides to get } a : b.$$

$$\frac{a^2}{b^2} = \frac{36}{25} \qquad \text{Square both sides to get } a^2 : b^2.$$

Ratio of surface areas $= 36 : 25$

If the larger pyramid has surface area 250 in.^{2}, let the smaller pyramid have surface area x. Then

$$\frac{250}{x} = \frac{36}{25}$$

$$36x = 6250$$

$$x \approx 173.6 \text{ in.}^2$$

Exercises

Find the similarity ratio.

1. Similar cylinders have volumes of 200π in.^{3} and 25π in.^{3}

2. Similar cylinders have surface areas of 45π in.^{2} and 20π in.^{2}

Find the ratio of volumes.

3. Two cubes have sides of length 4 cm and 5 cm.

4. Two cubes have surface areas of 64 in.^{2} and 25 in.^{2}

5. Similar pyramids have bases with areas of 50 in.^{2} and 9 in.^{2}

Find the ratio of surface areas.

6. Two cubes have volumes of 64 cm^3 and 27 cm^3.

7. Similar cylinders have volumes of 343π cm^3 and 125π cm^3.

Practice 10-8

Areas and Volumes of Similar Solids

The figures in each pair are similar. Use the given information to find the
similarity ratio of the smaller figure to the larger figure.

1.

S.A. = 49 cm^2 S.A. = 81 cm^2

2.

V = 125 in.^{3} V = 512 in.^{3}

Are the two solids in each pair similar? If so, give the similarity ratio. If not,
write *not similar*.

3.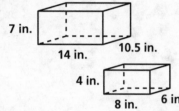

7 in.

14 in.   10.5 in.

4 in.

8 in.   6 in.

4.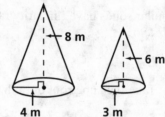

8 m

6 m

4 m   3 m

5.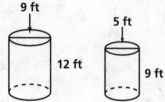

9 ft

5 ft

12 ft

9 ft

6.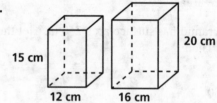

20 cm

15 cm

12 cm   16 cm

The surface areas of two similar figures are given. The volume of the larger
figure is given. Find the volume of the smaller figure.

7. S.A. = 25 cm^2
S.A. = 36 cm^2
V = 216 cm^3

8. S.A. = 16 in.^{2}
S.A. = 25 in.^{2}
V = 500 in.^{3}

9. S.A. = 72 ft^2
S.A. = 98 ft^2
V = 686 ft^3

The volumes of two similar figures are given. The surface area of the smaller
figure is given. Find the surface area of the larger figure.

10. V = 8 ft^3
V = 125 ft^3
S.A. = 4 ft^2

11. V = 40 m^3
V = 135 m^3
S.A. = 40 m^2

12. V = 125 cm^3
V = 1000 cm^3
S.A. = 150 cm^2

13. A cone-shaped pile of sand weighs 250 lb. How much does a similarly
shaped pile of sand weigh if each dimension is six times as large?

14. A block of ice weighs 2 lb. How much does a similarly shaped block of
ice weigh if each dimension is twice as large?

Reteaching 11-1

OBJECTIVE: Finding the relationship between a radius and a tangent and between two tangents drawn from the same point

MATERIALS: None

Example

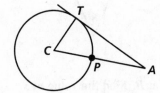

$\overline{AT}$ is tangent to $\odot C$ at T.
$\overline{AT}$ is twice as long as $\overline{AP}$.
$\odot C$ has radius 3.
Find AP and AT.

Because $\overline{AT}$ is tangent at T, $\angle ATC$ is a right angle. Therefore, by the Pythagorean Theorem,

$$AT^2 + CT^2 = AC^2$$
$$AT^2 + CT^2 = (CP + AP)^2$$

Because $AT = 2AP$, $(2AP)^2 + CT^2 = (CP + AP)^2$.

And because radius $= 3$, $(2AP)^2 + 9 = (3 + AP)^2$.

Now solve for AP.

$$4AP^2 + 9 = 9 + 6AP + AP^2$$
$$3AP^2 - 6AP = 0$$
$$3AP(AP - 2) = 0$$
$$AP = 0 \text{ or } AP = 2$$

Because $AP > 0$, $AP = 2$, and $AT = 4$.

Exercises

Find the measure of each segment.

1. $\odot C$ has radius 6. From point Q outside $\odot C$, a tangent is drawn meeting $\odot C$ at point T. $QT = 11$. Find QC.

2. Point X lies outside $\odot W$. $XW = 29$. $\odot W$ has radius 10. A tangent is drawn from X to $\odot W$, meeting the circle at point T. Find XT.

3. $\odot M$ has radius 4. From external point E, a tangent is drawn meeting $\odot M$ at T. $\overline{ET}$ has length $\frac{1}{3}$ the length of $\overline{EM}$. Find ET.

4. From point B, a tangent is drawn to $\odot C$, meeting it at T. $\overline{BC}$ meets the circle at X. $BX = 5$ and $BT = 10$. Find the radius of $\odot C$.

Practice 11-1

Assume that lines that appear to be tangent are tangent. *C* is the center of each circle. Find the value of *x*.

1.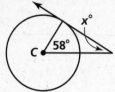

2.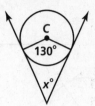

3.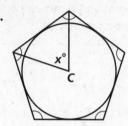

In each diagram, $\overrightarrow{AB}$ is tangent to ⊙*C* at *B*. Find the value of *x*.

4.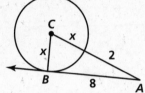

5.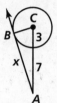

6.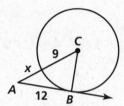

In each diagram, $\overleftrightarrow{ZY}$ is tangent to circles *O* and *P*. Find the value of *x*.

7.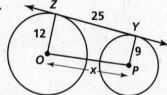

8.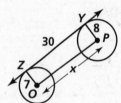

9.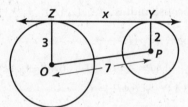

Tell whether each polygon is inscribed in or circumscribed about the circle.

10.

11.

12.

In each diagram, a polygon circumscribes a circle. Find the perimeter of each polygon.

13.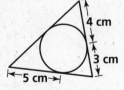

14.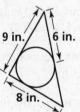

15.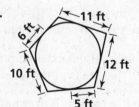

Reteaching 11-2

OBJECTIVE: Finding the lengths of chords and measures of arcs of a circle	MATERIALS: Calculator

Example

In $\odot C$, chord $\overline{AB}$ has length 16 cm and is 6 cm from the center.

Find the radius of $\odot C$ and $m\overset{\frown}{AB}$.

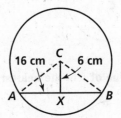

Draw $\overline{CX} \perp \overline{AB}$. By Theorem 11-6, $\overline{CX}$ bisects $\overline{AB}$. Therefore, $AX = 8$ cm. By the Pythagorean Theorem,

$$CX^2 + AX^2 = CA^2$$
$$6^2 + 8^2 = CA^2$$
$$100 = CA^2$$
$$10 \text{ cm} = CA$$

To find $m\overset{\frown}{AB}$, first extend $\overline{CX}$, as shown at the right. By Theorem 11-6, $\overline{CM}$ bisects $\overset{\frown}{AB}$. So, $m\overset{\frown}{AB} = 2m\overset{\frown}{AM} = 2m\angle ACX$.

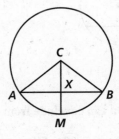

Then use trigonometry to find $m\angle ACX$.

$$\tan(\angle ACX) = \frac{AX}{CX} = \frac{8}{6} = 1.3\overline{3}$$
$$m\angle ACX = 53.1$$
$$\text{So } m\overset{\frown}{AB} = 106.2$$

Exercises

Find x using the information given. Leave your answers in simplest radical form.

1.

$AB = 20$
radius = 15
$CM = x$

2.

$AB = 24$
$CP = 12$
$CA = x$

3.

$CP = 5$
radius = 9
$AB = x$

Find the measure of each segment to the nearest hundredth.

4. Find the length of a chord that is 1 cm from the center of a circle of radius 6 cm.

5. Find the length of a chord that is 8 cm from the center of a circle of radius 8.1 cm.

6. For a circle of radius 10 in., find the distance from the center to a chord of length 10 in.

7. For a circle of radius 8 in., find the distance from the center to a chord of length 15 in.

Practice 11-2

Find the radius and $m\widehat{AB}$.

1.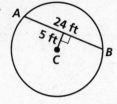

2.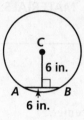

3.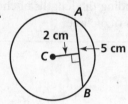

Find the value of *x* to the nearest tenth.

4.

5.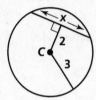

6.

7.

8.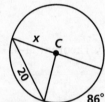

9.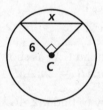

List what you can conclude from each diagram.

10. $\odot Q \cong \odot T,\ \widehat{PR} \cong \widehat{SU}$

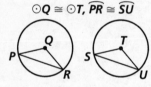

11. $\odot A \cong \odot J,\ \overline{BC} \cong \overline{KL}$

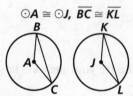

Write a two-column proof, a paragraph proof, or a flow proof.

12. Prove Theorem 11-5, part (2).

Given: $\odot O,\ \overline{OE} \perp \overline{AB},\ \overline{OF} \perp \overline{CD},\ AB = CD$

Prove: $OE = OF$

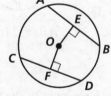

13. Given: $\odot O$ with $m\widehat{AB} = m\widehat{BC} = m\widehat{CA}$

Prove: $m\angle ABC = m\angle BCA = m\angle CAB$

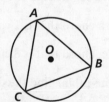

Reteaching 11-3

OBJECTIVE: Finding the measures of inscribed angles and the arcs they intercept	**MATERIALS:** None

Example

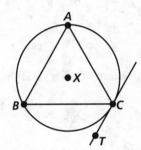

$\triangle ABC$ is isosceles with $AB = AC$ and is inscribed in $\odot X$. $\overline{CT}$ is tangent to $\odot X$ at point C. $m\widehat{AB} = 140$. Find $m\angle A$, $m\widehat{BC}$, and $m\angle BCT$.

$\angle ACB$ is inscribed in $\odot X$ and intercepts $\widehat{AB}$, so $m\angle ACB = \frac{1}{2}m\widehat{AB} = \frac{1}{2}(140) = 70$. And because $AB = AC$, $m\angle B = m\angle ACB = 70$. So $m\angle A = 180 - 70 - 70 = 40$, and $m\widehat{BC} = 2m\angle A = 80$.

Finally, $\angle BCT$ is an angle formed by a chord and tangent. Therefore, by Theorem 11-10,

$$m\angle BCT = \frac{1}{2}m\widehat{BC} = 40.$$

Exercises

Find the value of each variable.

1.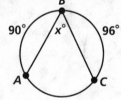

2.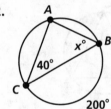

3.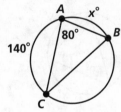

4.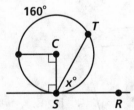

5.

6.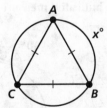

Points A, B, and D lie on $\odot C$. $m\angle ACB = 40$. $m\widehat{AB} < m\widehat{AD}$. Find each measure.

7. $m\widehat{AB}$

8. $m\angle ADB$

9. $m\angle BAC$

Practice 11-3

For each diagram, indicate a pair of congruent inscribed angles.

1.

2.

3.

Find the value of each variable.

4.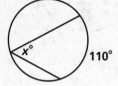

5.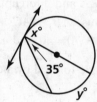

6.

7.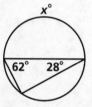

8.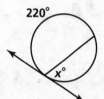

9.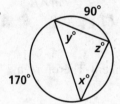

10.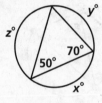

11.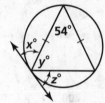

12.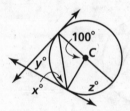

Find each indicated measure for ⊙O.

13. a. $m\widehat{AE}$
    b. $m\angle C$
    c. $m\angle BEC$
    d. $m\angle D$

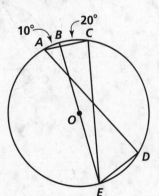

14. a. $m\angle A$
    b. $m\angle B$
    c. $m\angle C$
    d. $m\angle D$

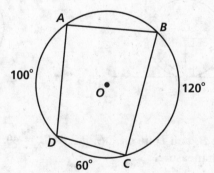

Reteaching 11-4

Angle Measures and Segment Lengths

OBJECTIVE: Finding the measures of angles formed by chords, secants, and tangents	MATERIALS: None

Example

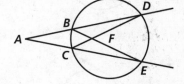

In the circle shown, $m\widehat{BC} = 15$ and $m\widehat{DE} = 35$.

Find $m\angle A$ and $m\angle BFC$.

Because $\overleftrightarrow{AD}$ and $\overleftrightarrow{AE}$ are secants, $m\angle A$ can be found using Theorem 11-11, part (2).

$$m\angle A = \tfrac{1}{2}(m\widehat{DE} - m\widehat{BC})$$
$$= \tfrac{1}{2}(35 - 15)$$
$$= 10$$

Because $\overline{BE}$ and $\overline{CD}$ are chords, $m\angle BFC$ can be found using Theorem 11-11, part (1).

$$m\angle BFC = \tfrac{1}{2}(m\widehat{DE} + m\widehat{BC})$$
$$= \tfrac{1}{2}(35 + 15)$$
$$= 25$$

Exercises

Find the value of each variable.

1.
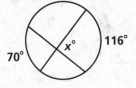

2.
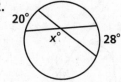

3.

4.
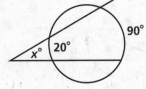

5.
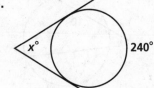

6.
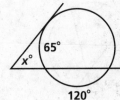

7.
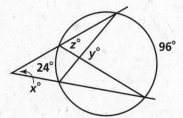

8.
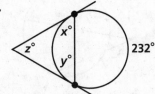

9.
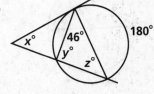

Practice 11-4

Angle Measures and Segment Lengths

Find the value of *x*.

1.
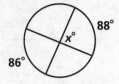

2.
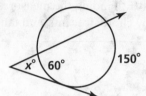

3.
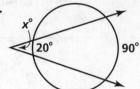

4.
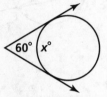

5.
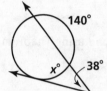

6.
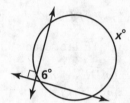

Algebra **Find the value of each variable using the given chords, secants, and tangents. If your answer is not a whole number, round it to the nearest tenth.**

7.
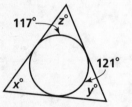

8.
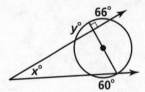

9.
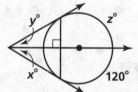

10.
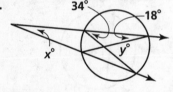

11.
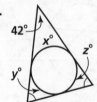

12.
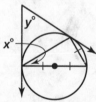

13.
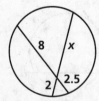

14.
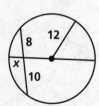

15.
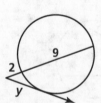

16.
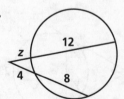

17.
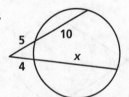

18.
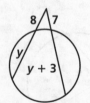

Reteaching 11-5

Circles in the Coordinate Plane

OBJECTIVE: Writing the equation of a circle	**MATERIALS:** None

Example

Find the equation of the circle whose center is $(-5, 2)$ and that passes through $(3, 3)$.

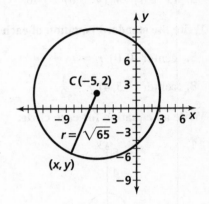

Use the center and point to find the radius.

$r = \sqrt{(-5 - 3)^2 + (2 - 3)^2}$ Distance Formula
$r = \sqrt{(-8)^2 + (-1)^2}$
$r = \sqrt{65}$

With $r = \sqrt{65}$ and center at $(-5, 2)$, the circle has the equation

$(x - (-5))^2 + (y - 2)^2 = (\sqrt{65})^2$.

Simplified, this becomes $(x + 5)^2 + (y - 2)^2 = 65$.

Exercises

Find the equation of the circle whose center and radius are given.

1. center $(3, 11)$
radius = 2

2. center $(-5, 0)$
radius = 15

3. center $(6, -6)$
radius = $\sqrt{7}$

Find the equation of the circle that passes through the point $(-2, -4)$ with the given center.

4. $C(0, 0)$

5. $C(-2, -2)$

6. $C(3, 1)$

Find the equation of each circle described.

7. The circle has center $(5, 2)$ and diameter 12.

8. The endpoints of the circle's diameter are the points $(4, -3)$ and $(4, 7)$.

9. The endpoints of the circle's diameter are the points $(2, 6)$ and $(-6, 0)$.

Identify the center and radius of each circle.

10. $(x + 3)^2 + (y + 5)^2 = 25$

11. $x^2 + y^2 = 0.04$

12. $(x - 4)^2 + y^2 = 6$

13. $\frac{(x - 3)^2}{2} + \frac{(y - 5)^2}{2} = 8$

Practice 11-5

Circles in the Coordinate Plane

Find the center and radius of each circle.

1. $x^2 + y^2 = 36$

2. $(x - 2)^2 + (y - 7)^2 = 49$

3. $(x + 1)^2 + (y + 6)^2 = 16$

4. $(x + 3)^2 + (y - 11)^2 = 12$

Write the standard equation of each circle.

5. center $(0, 0)$; $r = 7$

6. center $(4, 3)$; $r = 8$

7. center $(5, 3)$; $r = 2$

8. center $(-5, 4)$; $r = \frac{1}{2}$

9. center $(-2, -5)$; $r = \sqrt{2}$

10. center $(-1, 6)$; $r = \sqrt{5}$

Write an equation for each circle.

11.

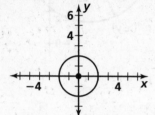

12.

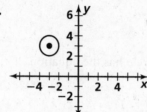

13.

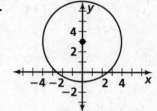

14.

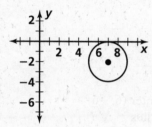

15.

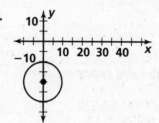

16.

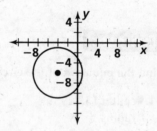

Graph each circle. Label its center, and state its radius.

17. $x^2 + y^2 = 25$

18. $(x - 3)^2 + (y - 5)^2 = 9$

19. $(x + 2)^2 + (y + 4)^2 = 16$

20. $(x + 1)^2 + (y - 1)^2 = 36$

Write an equation for each circle with the given center that passes through the given point.

21. center $(0, 0)$; point $(3, 4)$

22. center $(5, 9)$; point $(2, 9)$

23. center $(-4, -3)$; point $(2, 2)$

24. center $(7, -2)$; point $(-1, -6)$

Write an equation that describes the position and range of each circle.

25. $\odot B$

26. $\odot F$

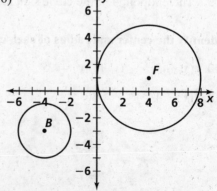

Geometry Chapter 11

Reteaching 11-6

Locus

OBJECTIVE: Using perpendicular bisectors to solve locus problems	MATERIALS: Compass, straightedge

Example

A family on vacation wants to hike on Oak Mountain and fish at North Pond and along the White River. Where on the river should they fish in order to be equidistant from North Pond and Oak Mountain?

Draw a line segment joining North Pond and Oak Mountain.

Construct the perpendicular bisector of that segment.

The family should fish where the perpendicular bisector meets the White River.

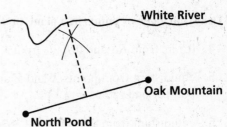

Exercises

Describe each of the following, and then compare your answers with those of a partner.

1. the locus of points equidistant from your desk and your partner's desk

2. the locus of points on the floor equidistant from the two side walls of your classroom

3. the locus of points equidistant from a window and the door of your classroom

4. the locus of points equidistant from the front and back walls of your classroom

5. the locus of points equidistant from the floor and the ceiling of your classroom

Use points A and B to complete the following.

6. Describe the locus of points in a plane equidistant from points A and B. $A \bullet$

7. How many points are equidistant from A and B and also lie on $\overleftrightarrow{AB}$? Explain your reasoning. $\bullet B$

Practice 11-6

Draw each locus of points in a plane.

1. 1.5 cm from point T • T

2. 1 in. from $\overline{PQ}$ P •————————• Q

3. equidistant from the endpoints of $\overline{AB}$ A •————————• B

Draw the locus of points in a plane that satisfy the given conditions.

4. 0.5 in. from $\overline{RS}$ and 0.75 in. from S, where $RS = 2.5$ in.

5. equidistant from points X and Y and on a circle with center at point X and radius $= \frac{1}{2}XY$

6. equidistant from the sides of $\angle ABC$ and on $\odot E$

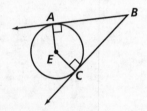

7. equidistant from both points F and G and points H and J

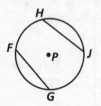

Describe each locus.

8. the set of points in a plane equidistant from two parallel lines

9. the set of points in space a given distance from a point

10. the set of points in a plane less than 1 in. from a given point

Sketch and label each locus.

11. all points in a plane 2 cm from a point Q

12. all points in a plane 0.75 in. from a line $\overleftrightarrow{RS}$

13. all points in space 0.5 cm from a segment $\overline{TU}$

14. all points in a plane 6 mm from a circle with radius 5 mm

Reteaching 12-1

Reflections

OBJECTIVE: Locating reflection images of figures	**MATERIALS:** Scissors, graph paper

Example

Find the reflection images of △*MNO* in the *x*- and *y*-axes.
Give the coordinates of the vertices of the images.

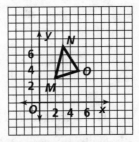

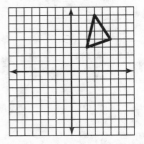

Copy the figure onto
a piece of graph paper.

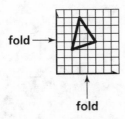

Fold the paper along
the *x*-axis and *y*-axis.

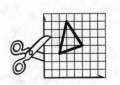

Cut out the triangle.

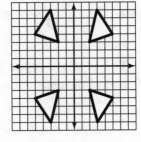

Unfold the paper.

From the graph we can see that the reflection image of △*MNO* in the *x*-axis
has vertices at $(2, -3), (3, -7),$ and $(5, -4)$. The reflection image of △*MNO*
in the *y*-axis has vertices at $(-2, 3), (-3, 7),$ and $(-5, 4)$.

Exercises

Use a sheet of graph paper to complete Exercises 1–5.

1. Draw and label the *x*- and *y*-axes on a sheet of graph paper.

2. Draw a nonregular triangle in one of the four quadrants. Make sure
   that the vertices are on the intersection of grid lines.

3. Fold the paper along the axes.

4. Cut out the triangle, and unfold the paper.

5. Label the coordinates of the vertices of the reflection images in the
   x- and *y*-axes.

**Find the coordinates of the vertices for the reflection images of the triangle
in the *x*- and *y*-axes.**

6. △*FGH* with vertices $F(-1, 3), G(-5, 1), H(-3, 5)$

7. △*CDE* with vertices $C(2, 4), D(5, 2), E(6, 3)$

8. △*JKL* with vertices $J(-1, -5), K(-2, -3), L(-4, -6)$

Practice 12-1

Reflections

Use the figures to complete Exercises 1–5.

1. For figure *IJKL*, draw its reflection image in each line.
   a. *x*-axis
   b. *y*-axis

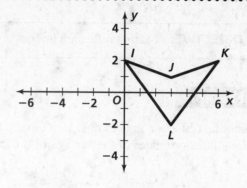

2. In the diagram, *C'D'E'F'* is the image of *CDEF.*
   a. Name the images of ∠*C* and ∠*F.*
   b. List the pairs of corresponding sides.

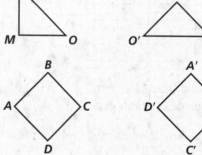

3. In the diagram, *M'N'O'* is the image of *MNO.*
   a. Name the images of ∠*M* and ∠*N.*
   b. List the pairs of corresponding sides.

4. *A'B'C'D'* is the image of *ABCD.*
   a. Name the images of ∠*A* and ∠*C.*
   b. List the pairs of corresponding sides.

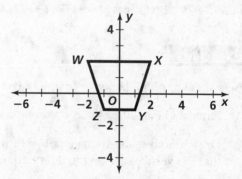

5. For figure *WXYZ*, draw its reflection image in each line.
   a. *x*-axis
   b. *y*-axis

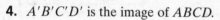

State whether each transformation appears to be an isometry. Explain.

6.

7.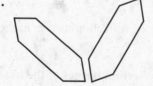

8.

Given points *T*(2, 4), *A*(−3, −4), and *B*(0, −4), draw △*TAB* and its reflection image in each line.

9. *x*-axis

10. *y*-axis

11. *x* = −3

12. *y* = 4

Geometry Chapter 12

Reteaching 12-2

OBJECTIVE: Using vectors to represent translations

MATERIALS: Graph paper, scissors, tracing paper

Example

What vector describes the translation of $ABCD$ to $A'B'C'D'$?

To get from A to A' (or from B to B' or C to C'), you move eight units left and seven units down. The vector that describes this translation is $\langle -8, -7 \rangle$.

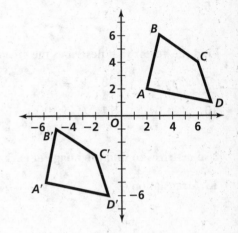

Exercises

- On graph paper, draw the x- and y-axes, and label Quadrants I–IV.

- Draw a quadrilateral in Quadrant I. Make sure that the vertices are on the intersection of grid lines.

- Trace the quadrilateral, and cut it out.

- Use the cutout to translate the figure to each of the other three quadrants.

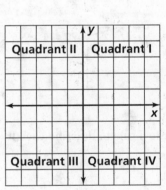

Name the vector that describes each translation of your quadrilateral.

1. from Quadrant I to Quadrant II

2. from Quadrant I to Quadrant III

3. from Quadrant I to Quadrant IV

4. from Quadrant II to Quadrant III

5. from Quadrant III to Quadrant I

Refer to $ABCD$ in the example above.

6. Give the coordinates of the image of $ABCD$ under the translation $\langle -2, -5 \rangle$.

7. Give the coordinates of the image of $ABCD$ under the translation $\langle 2, -4 \rangle$.

8. Give the coordinates of the image of $ABCD$ under the translation $\langle 1, 3 \rangle$.

Practice 12-2

Translations

• •

What is the image of Z under each translation?

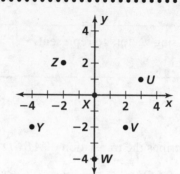

1. $\langle 2, -2 \rangle$

2. $\langle 5, -1 \rangle$

3. $\langle 2, -6 \rangle$

4. $\langle 4, -4 \rangle$

5. $\langle 0, 0 \rangle$

6. $\langle -2, -4 \rangle$

Find the vector that describes the given translation.

7. $Z \rightarrow Y$ **8.** $V \rightarrow W$ **9.** $U \rightarrow X$

10. $Y \rightarrow W$ **11.** $U \rightarrow Z$ **12.** $W \rightarrow V$

Use matrices to find the image of each figure under the given translation.

13. translation $\langle 2, 4 \rangle$ **14.** translation $\langle -2, 1 \rangle$ **15.** translation $\langle 5, -3 \rangle$

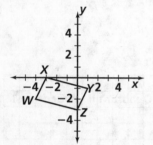 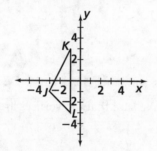 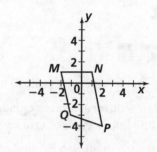

Write a rule to describe each translation.

16.   **17.**   **18.**

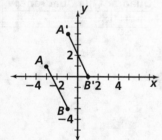 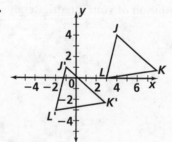 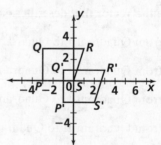

Find a single translation that has the same effect as each composition of translations.

19. $\langle 3, 5.2 \rangle$ followed by $\langle 1.2, 6 \rangle$ **20.** $\langle 4, -8 \rangle$ followed by $\langle 9, -5 \rangle$

21. $\langle 7, 11 \rangle$ followed by $\langle -7, -11 \rangle$ **22.** $\langle 1, 2 \rangle$ followed by $\langle 2, 1 \rangle$

23. $\triangle PNQ$ has vertices $P(2, 5)$, $N(-3, -1)$, and $Q(4, 0)$.

     a. Determine the image of P under the translation $\langle -5, -6 \rangle$.

     b. Use matrices to find the image of $\triangle PNQ$ under the translation $\langle -2, 3 \rangle$.

Reteaching 12-3

OBJECTIVE: Locating rotation images of figures	**MATERIALS:** Protractor, compass

Example

Draw the image of △*CAT* under a 60° rotation about *P*.

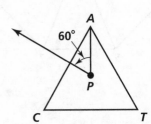

Step 1: Use a protractor to draw a 60° angle with side $\overline{PA}$.

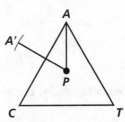

Step 2: Use a compass to construct $\overline{PA} \cong \overline{PA'}$.

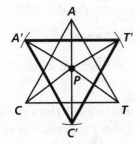

Step 3: Create *C'* and *T'* in a similar manner. Draw △*C'A'T'*.

Exercises

Complete the following steps to draw the image of △*XYZ* under a 80° rotation about *T*.

1. Draw ∠*XTX'* so that *m*∠*XTX'* = 80° and $\overline{TX} \cong \overline{TX'}$.

2. Trace △*XYZ*, $\overline{TX}$, and $\overline{TX'}$.

3. Place your tracing under the triangle at the right so that the two triangles and point *T* align.

4. With your pencil on *T*, rotate $\overline{TX'}$ on this paper until it is on top of $\overline{TX}$ on your tracing.

5. Trace the triangle from your tracing onto this paper, and label it △*X'Y'Z'*.

Use the image above to complete Exercises 6–8.

6. Draw the image of △*XYZ* under a 120° rotation about *T*.

7. Draw a point *S* inside △*XYZ*. Draw the image of △*XYZ* under a 135° rotation about *S*.

8. Draw the image of △*XYZ* under a 90° rotation about *Y*.

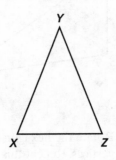

Practice 12-3

Rotations

Regular octagon *EIGHTSUP* is divided into eight congruent triangles.
Find the image of each point or segment for the given rotation.

1. 45° rotation of *G* about *Z*

2. 225° rotation of *U* about *Z*

3. 315° rotation of *E* about *Z*

4. 270° rotation of $\overline{EI}$ about *Z*

5. 135° rotation of *S* about *Z*

6. 360° rotation of $\overline{ST}$ about *Z*

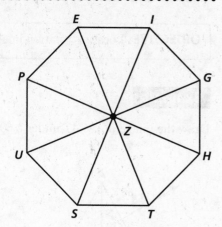

**Copy each figure and point *P*. Draw the image of each figure for the given
rotation about *P*. Label the vertices of each image.**

7. 70°

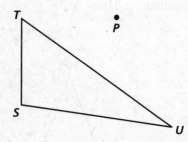

8. 50°

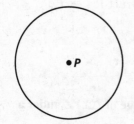

9. 90°

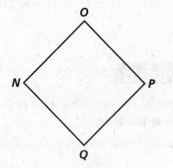

10. Rotate the hexagon 60° about point *E*, draw its image, and label the
    vertices. Repeat this procedure three more times, rotating the original
    figure 120°, 180°, and 240°.

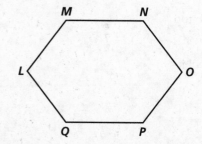

11. In Exercise 10, which vertex is closest to point *E* in all four figures?

**Copy △*PQR* and point *S*. Then draw the image for the given composition
of rotations about point *S*.**

12. 20° and then 70°

13. 30° and then 30°

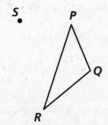

Reteaching 12-4

OBJECTIVE: Identifying reflections and their relation to other isometries	**MATERIALS:** None

Example

Name a transformation that maps the figure *ABCD* onto the figure *EFGH* shown at the right.

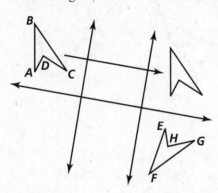

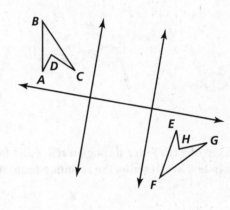

The transformation is a glide reflection. It involves a translation, or glide, followed by a reflection in a line parallel to the translation vector.

Exercises

- Draw two pairs of parallel lines that intersect as shown at the right.

- Draw a nonregular quadrilateral in the center of the four lines.

- Use paper folding and tracing to reflect the figure and its images so that there is a figure in each of the nine sections.

- Label the figures 1 through 9 as shown.

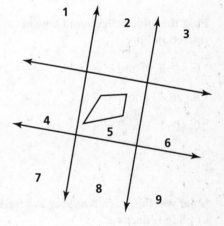

Describe a transformation that maps each of the following.

1. figure 4 onto figure 6

2. figure 1 onto figure 2

3. figure 7 onto figure 5

4. figure 2 onto figure 9

5. figure 1 onto figure 5

6. figure 6 onto figure 7

7. figure 8 onto figure 9

8. figure 2 onto figure 8

Practice 12-4

Compositions of Reflections

Match each image of the figure at the left with one of the following
isometries: **A.** reflection **B.** rotation **C.** translation **D.** glide reflection.

1. PUSH→ I. ↑PUSH II. PUSH→ III. *PUSH→* IV. ←HƧUꟼ

2. 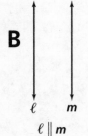 I. [glasses image] II. [glasses image] III. [glasses image] IV. [glasses image]

Find the image of each letter through a reflection in line *l* and then
a reflection in line *m*. Describe the resulting translation.

3.

B

l *m*

l ∥ *m*

4.

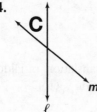

C

m

l

5.

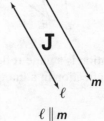

J

m

l

l ∥ *m*

Find the glide reflection image of △*BEST* for the given glide and
reflection line.

6. ⟨−2, 0⟩ and *x* = 0

7. ⟨0, −1⟩ and *y* = 2

8. ⟨0, 2⟩ and *x* = 2

9. ⟨2, 2⟩ and *y* = *x*

10. ⟨−1, 1⟩ and *y* = 0

11. ⟨2, 2⟩ and *y* = −*x*

12. ⟨0, 1⟩ and *x* = 0

13. ⟨1, 1⟩ and *y* = 0

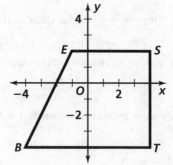

State whether each mapping is a reflection, rotation, translation,
or glide reflection.

14. △*ABCD* → △*GHCD*

15. △*HGJI* → △*LMJK*

16. △*GFED* → △*RQOP*

17. △*MNOP* → △*ABCD*

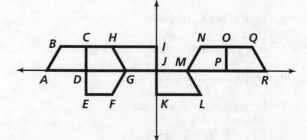

Reteaching 12-5

Symmetry

OBJECTIVE: Identifying types of symmetry in figures	**MATERIALS:** None

Consider the following types of symmetry: rotational, point, line, and reflectional.

Example

What types of symmetry does the flag have?

The flag has four lines of symmetry shown by the dotted lines. It has 90° rotational symmetry and point symmetry about its center.

Switzerland

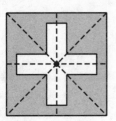

Exercises

Describe the symmetries in each flag.

1.

Israel

2.

South Africa

3.

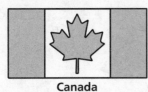

Canada

4.

United Kingdom

5.

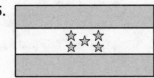

Honduras

6.

Somalia

Practice 12-5

Symmetry

Tell whether each three-dimensional object has rotational symmetry about
a line and/or reflectional symmetry in a plane.

1.

2.

3.

4.

Draw all lines of symmetry for each figure.

5.

6.

7.

Judging from appearance, tell what type(s) of symmetry each figure has.
If it has line symmetry, sketch the figure and the line(s) of symmetry.
If it has rotational symmetry, state the angle of rotation.

8.

9.

10.

11.

12.

13. BOOK

14.

15.

16.

Each diagram shows a figure folded along a line of symmetry. Sketch the
unfolded figure.

17.

18.

19.

20.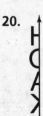

21.

Name _____ Class _____ Date _____

Reteaching 12-6

OBJECTIVE: Identifying symmetries of tessellations

MATERIALS: Stiff paper or cardboard, scissors

Example

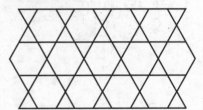

List the symmetries of the tessellation.

The tessellation has line symmetry as shown by the dotted lines below. It has rotational symmetry about the points shown. It has translational symmetry and glide reflection symmetry.

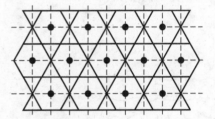

Exercises

Copy the figure at the right onto stiff paper or cardboard. Then cut it out.

1. Use the cutout to create a tessellation.

2. List the symmetries of the tessellation.

List the symmetries of each tessellation.

3.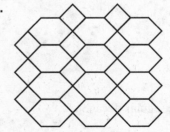

4.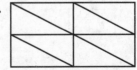

5.

Practice 12-6

Describe the symmetries of each tessellation. Copy a portion of the tessellation, and draw any centers of rotational symmetry or lines of symmetry.

1.

2.
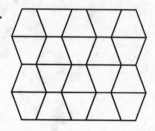

3.
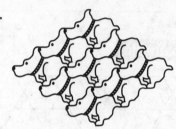

4.

5.
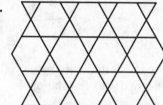

6.
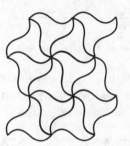

Identify the repeating figure or figures that make up each tessellation.

7.
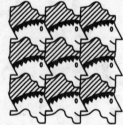

8.

Use each figure to create a tessellation on dot paper.

9.
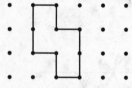

10.
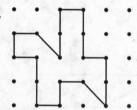

11.
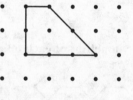

Determine whether each figure will tessellate a plane.

12. rhombus

13. acute triangle

14. regular decagon

15. regular hexagon

16. regular dodecagon

17. regular 15-gon

Reteaching 12-7

Dilations

| **OBJECTIVE:** Locating dilation images of figures | **MATERIALS:** Graph paper |

Example

Quadrilateral $ABCD$ has vertices $A(-2, 0)$, $B(0, 2)$, $C(2, 0)$, and $D(0, -2)$. Find the image of $ABCD$ under the dilation centered at the origin with scale factor 2. Then graph $ABCD$ and its image.

To find the image of the vertices of $ABCD$, multiply the x-coordinates and y-coordinates by 2.

$A(-2, 0) \rightarrow A'(-4, 0)$ $B(0, 2) \rightarrow B'(0, 4)$

$C(2, 0) \rightarrow C'(4, 0)$ $D(0, -2) \rightarrow D'(0, -4)$

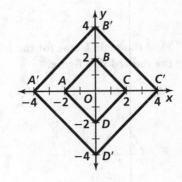

Exercises

Use graph paper to complete Exercise 1.

1. **a.** Draw a quadrilateral in the coordinate plane.

   b. Draw the image of the quadrilateral under dilations centered at the origin with scale factors $\frac{1}{2}$, 2, and 4.

Draw the image of each figure under a dilation centered at the origin with the given scale factor.

2.

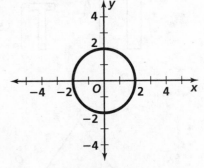

scale factor 2

3.

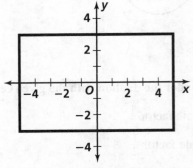

scale factor $\frac{1}{2}$

4.

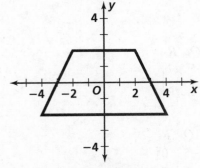

scale factor 3

5.

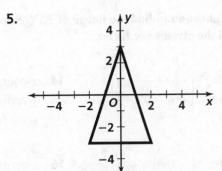

scale factor 4

Practice 12-7

Dilations

Use matrices to find the image of figure *LMNO* under a dilation centered
at the origin with the given scale factor.

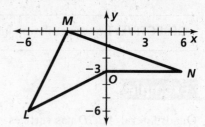

1. $\frac{1}{3}$ **2.** 5   **3.** 2

Find the scale factor for the dilation that maps the solid-line figure onto
the dashed-line figure.

4.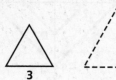

5.

6.

For each pair of figures, determine whether one figure is a dilation of
the other.

7.

8.

9.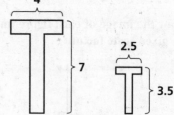

Draw △*A'R'T'* under the dilation with the given center and scale factor.

10. center *O*, scale factor $\frac{1}{2}$

11. center *T*, scale factor $\frac{1}{2}$

12. center *O*, scale factor 2

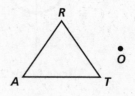

Use scalar multiplication to find the image of △*PQR* for a dilation with
center (0, 0) and the given scale factor.

13. *x*-coordinate $\begin{array}{ccc} P & Q & R \end{array}$
y-coordinate $\begin{bmatrix} -6 & -3 & 0 \\ -6 & 0 & -3 \end{bmatrix}$
scale factor 2

14. *x*-coordinate $\begin{array}{ccc} P & Q & R \end{array}$
y-coordinate $\begin{bmatrix} -2 & 5 & 7 \\ 1 & -1 & 8 \end{bmatrix}$
scale factor $\frac{1}{4}$

15. *x*-coordinate $\begin{array}{ccc} P & Q & R \end{array}$
y-coordinate $\begin{bmatrix} -7 & 1 & -2 \\ 2 & 8 & 2 \end{bmatrix}$
scale factor 3

16. *x*-coordinate $\begin{array}{ccc} P & Q & R \end{array}$
y-coordinate $\begin{bmatrix} -10 & -5 & 0 \\ 5 & 0 & 5 \end{bmatrix}$
scale factor $\frac{1}{5}$